Ideas for Librarians Who Teach

With Suggestions for Teachers and Business Presenters

Naomi Lederer

The Scarecrow Press, Inc.
Lanham, Maryland • Toronto • Oxford
2005

SCARECROW PRESS, INC.

Published in the United States of America
by Scarecrow Press, Inc.
A wholly owned subsidiary of
The Rowman & Littlefield Publishing Group, Inc.
4501 Forbes Boulevard, Suite 200, Lanham, Maryland 20706
www.scarecrowpress.com

PO Box 317
Oxford
OX2 9RU, UK

British Library Cataloguing in Publication Information Available

Library of Congress Cataloging-in-Publication Data
Lederer, Naomi, 1965-
  Ideas for librarians who teach : with suggestions for teachers and business
presenters / Naomi Lederer.
     p. cm.
  Includes bibliographical references and index.
  ISBN 0-8108-5212-8 (pbk. : alk. paper)
  1. Library orientation--Handbooks, manuals, etc. I. Title.
Z711.2.L435 2005
025.5'6--dc22   2005019736

⊖™ The paper used in this publication meets the minimum requirements of
American National Standard for Information Sciences—Permanence of
Paper for Printed Library Materials, ANSI/NISO Z39.48-1992.
Manufactured in the United States of America.

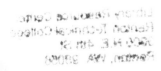

For Leslie, with love

Contents

Introduction

The purpose of this book is to provide a range of ideas that apply to teaching library instruction. Ideas have been generated from over sixteen years of my experience teaching library instruction (sometimes referred to as bibliographic instruction or BI). I have taught one-time (50-minute to three-hour) sessions; two sessions for the same section; semester- and half-semester-long library research credit courses (both in the traditional classroom and on live cable television); a graduate library science course in bibliography; non-credit library research classes; as the sole librarian teacher and as part of a team; and have been a guest speaker on WebCT using PowerPoint (creating the library-related assignment that went with the lecture) with audio.

In addition to thinking about my experiences and recalling conversations, I read numerous books and articles about teaching, speaking, learning styles, and more, aimed at librarians and others. There are fabulous resources available from the fields of education and business. These fields have extraordinarily good ideas that apply to the teacher librarian. Moreover, these are experts who either teach every day and have had formal courses on how to teach, or have enormous consequences riding on the outcome. A business presenter may have millions of dollars on the line (or his or her job, for that matter) when speaking, so the stakes are much higher than the stakes for a librarian, so why not learn from those who must give good presentations or risk losing their jobs?

Teachers and business presenters are included in the title of the book because many of the ideas will be useful to them. Teachers might find chapters 4-5 and 7-14 the most useful; business presenters will be most interested in chapters 3-5, 7-8, and 10. Other chapters have tips for these readers, but if time is short they will probably want to go immediately to what is of most use. This will apply to librarians also. While the book can be read from the beginning to the end, a librarian may be specifically interested in visuals, or wish to get some ideas that will apply to questions in the classroom, and he or she can jump right to what is needed at that moment and read other sections later.

A number of excellent theory books have been published, but this book focuses on the practical. A few of the ideas are the same idea said differently. Others ideas may even contradict one another. My hope is that when a librarian (or teacher) needs some teaching ideas, this book will provide a number of them quickly. Nearly every tip is designed to have enough information to be immediately applied. No further research is necessary. Nevertheless, the reader who wants more details will find notes at the end of each chapter with resources that can be consulted for further information.

Teaching library instruction can be very rewarding. It can also be frustrating and challenging. Teaching the same information to different groups of uninterested (or outright hostile) students over and over can be discouraging. Can you say Web site for Speech 200? I can! The instructors for the course use the Web site—it gets plenty of hits. The library even gets three pages in their course textbook where there is strategy advice and promotion of the Web site created for their specific assignments. When I was the first-year composition liaison, with the strict understanding that my colleagues were at that point fed up with teaching sections of the course, I created a Web site on library research in conjunction with the then head of the program. (See my "New Form(at)" article for a description of how the site used to be.) Mine is not the only way. The current liaison is creating online tutorials and teaching nearly every section of the course with the help of several colleagues. At my previous job I was able to get the library tour and a library research skills section into the first year composition book, updating the graduate teaching assistants and adjunct instructors every year. Information provided by a librarian in a textbook is library instruction. Web pages tied to courses are also library instruction.

The first two chapters of *Ideas for Librarians Who Teach* and the chapter on learning styles are the least "practical" chapters of the book, but they give some very useful information for any teacher to think about before teaching. It is important to consider your speaking style and nervous habits, and the librarian as key tool chapter describes how speakers are perceived by audiences and discusses ways to improve your speaking and movement. You are the key tool in the classroom—not the computer, and not your visuals. You. (There are some tips on combating stage fright.) Reading and talking about different learning styles has certainly changed my approach to the classroom.

The third chapter, on customizing, discusses ways to prepare for sessions, including what to ask the person requesting the presentation. Much of your teaching comes before you ever set foot in the classroom, while you are preparing for the session. The chapter on teaching in the classroom is the heart of the book. That is when you are in front of others and making an impact. In the diverse students and foreign teachers chapter, there are ideas for teaching foreigners (at home or abroad), being the foreigner teaching Americans, topics related to different learners, and reaching people with disabilities. Many of the ideas apply in general.

Classrooms can influence teachers and students. The classroom chapter talks about things to look for when teaching in an unfamiliar room and gives suggestions for things to request should you ever get to design a classroom from scratch. "Questions" addresses asking and answering questions while teaching—asking the students for feedback, and being asked by students for further explanations. Visuals get their own chapter; as the world becomes increasingly focused on what people see, it is important to use appropriate visuals. One major caveat—please do not use them (overheads, presentation software, etc.) just because they are there. In the library classroom when we are demonstrating library resources, we are already using visuals, so there is rarely a need to add to them. The chapter on Web pages talks about the usefulness of Web pages in the classroom, and gives some suggestions for creating them. Technical details are not provided here (there are plentiful sources on the free Web that can tell you how to use HTML, etc.), but there are some recommendations to get you started, and resources to consult once you have created or revised your page or site.

Handouts can be a very useful addition to a session, but they should be designed, not simply thrown together; the chapter on handouts gives reasons for handouts, what to include, and design recommendations. Humor in the classroom can be sticky, so there is chapter describing a few pitfalls—but also describes its uses. The chapter will not teach anyone how to be funny, but it should, at least, give everyone the confidence to use humor when possible.

The group learning chapter discusses pros and cons of group learning. Ways to create groups are covered and there are a few group configurations mentioned. For short one-time library sessions these are not necessarily going to be possible, but small groups of two or three can be effective in the library classroom. Teachers of regular classes will probably find this chapter more useful than other readers. On the other hand, there are probably some librarians who teach successfully doing nothing else. The option is always there. Do what works for you and your audience.

Becoming a better teacher is always desirable, and the chapter on evaluation and feedback describes some mechanisms for gathering comments on one's teaching. Sample evaluation forms are provided. Librarians can pick and choose what they think will be most meaningful and helpful to their situation, and adapt as wanted. Marketing a library instruction program can be a challenge, and the chapter on promoting it provides a wide range of ideas for getting the word out on what a librarian can provide for his or her constituents.

Distance education is a growing audience for librarians, and the chapter discusses teaching on television with a few ideas on other methods. Recent library science students and teachers who have nearly all of their courses online know more about the mechanisms of online courses, so they can be the experts on that topic. "Miscellaneous" picks up some pieces, such as dealing with complaints, a section on the dreaded burnout, and some ideas for teaching a credit library research course (with a syllabus that can be adapted to local use)—the ideas about being in the classroom from earlier chapters still apply.

In the hope that the utility of the book will be readily apparent, two syllabi and a workshop outline complete the book. One syllabus pretty much follows the sequence of this book, while the other emphasizes learning theory and works its way toward the practical. The workshop outline suggests ways the book can be used in a day or two-day workshop on library instruction (skip the theory; jump to what you can immediately apply). Of course, you should sequence any course or workshop you are offering in any way you wish.

I hope everyone who reads this book will find useful ideas. I wish you good luck in the classroom.

1

Knowing the Material

It is important that any speaker be comfortable with the content of the topic to be presented. Having a solid background knowledge of libraries and research skills should enable any librarian to teach with confidence. This brief chapter has some descriptions of effective teachers and what sorts of skills a librarian should posses.

1.1

It is essential that you be familiar with whatever topic you are teaching. By using your own collection and searching your own catalogs, indexes, and databases on an ongoing basis, you will have a practical awareness of what they can and cannot do. This knowledge will make you a more effective teacher.

1.2

"Students perform better when their teachers have majored or minored in the subject area they are teaching."[1] If you are going to be a school media specialist, please get a major or minor in library science. Two courses as part of an education degree will not make you an expert in library research (or in selecting materials or organizing your library). If you are already in the field, take continuing education courses on library topics and regularly read library science periodicals.

1.3

Knowing your material is critical if you are going to teach. If you cannot search your own library catalog you are going to look like a fool in front of your audience. On the other hand, when you have good, solid research skills and project this knowledge, if you do not have an immediate answer for every question, you will still be considered a reliable resource.

1.4
The school librarian can be a resource to improve the teaching skills of his or her colleagues. Circulate teaching tips, articles, and books that will help. Talk with your principal about these offerings. Some topics merit schoolwide or department wide discussion. Use this as an opportunity to promote and teach research skills to teachers. They need to learn library skills, too.

1.5
"Effective teachers recognize that no single instructional strategy an be used in all situations. Rather they develop and call on a broad repertoire of approaches that have proven successful for them with students of varying abilities, backgrounds, and interests."[2]

1.6
Keep up-to-date with the latest technologies. This is not only so you can demonstrate them, but so you will know what new equipment to request when funds are available.

1.7
Be aware of the larger topics of interest to your audience. If in a school, pay attention to teachers' and principals' curricular concerns. At the college level take note of required course and general graduation requirements. This allows you to address larger issue when teaching specific topics.

1.8
Read school papers and newsletters so your examples or introductory remarks can include relevant events and concerns.

1.9
Read library periodicals to see which innovations are being applied. In addition, these resources sometimes have recommended URLs for assorted topics.

1.10
Look through the periodicals read by your primary clientele—business, academic, science, and so forth. A glance at the tables of contents will help keep you familiar with issues of the day.

1.11
If you are not the expert, refer the presentation request to a colleague who is.

1.12
You can become the expert on many topics if given a long enough time to prepare. Consult the person requesting the session for key terms and ideas.

1.13
"In the current climate, written instruction, that is, print and Web-based support materials is becoming as just as important as face-to-face teaching to ensure that effective use is made of networked resources for everyday teaching and research. Distance education, online course delivery, and the permeation of electronic sources necessitates the flexible electronic delivery of information literacy. Therefore, librarians must develop skills in the areas of instructional design and Web publishing."[3]

1.14
In many cases, an academic librarian with a subject master's in addition to his or her library master's (professional) degree is seen as more credible by the teaching faculty and graduate students at the institution. An undergraduate degree in an academic subject is also valuable.

1.15
A librarian should know (or know immediately where to find this information on the library's Web site):
• Library hours, address, and/or building name, and key telephone numbers
• Names of subject specialists, administrators, and relevant staff members

1.16
A librarian should know how to:
• Search the library catalog
• Search all of the general indexes and abstracts—print and electronic
• Search subject indexes relevant to the session
• Find help screens in relevant databases
• Use the classroom equipment (computer, projectors, etc.) and sundries (open/shut blinds, etc.)

1.17
A librarian needs to know the differences between or among (and how to use):
• Indexes and abstracts
• General and subject encyclopedias
• Comprehensive and selective bibliographies
• Online library catalogs, online indexes/databases, and online reference resources
• Free and proprietary resources (particularly those accessible via the Web)

Notes

1.   James H. Stronge, *Qualities of Effective Teachers* (Alexandra, Va.: Association for Supervision and Curriculum Development, 2002), 8.
2.   Stronge, 45.
3.   Susie Moreton and Fiona Salisbury, "Staying on Top of the Heap: Information Literacy and Professional Development." http://elvis.cqu.edu.au/conference/2000/papers/moreton.htm (accessed December 24, 2003).

2

Librarian as Key Tool

The most important tool in the classroom is the teacher—not the equipment, the room, or the handouts. This chapter will give suggestions on how to present yourself, encourage you to show confidence, to dress appropriately, vary your voice, use gestures, combat stage fright, and not worry about giving perfect presentations.

2.1
Care about what you are doing. If you are indifferent to the results of your session, you will not be effective.

2.2
Project confidence. Act like you know what you are doing. Otherwise, why should anyone listen to you?

2.3
"Effective teachers' credibility and authenticity are enhanced when they deal with people humanely, honestly, fairly, and respectfully."[1]

2.4
Observe classes being taught before you teach. Not as a student, but as an observer. What do the librarians say? Do? Use? How do they interact with students? Call for and answer questions? Watch. Listen. Get ideas. How often do they use visual aids? How many example searches do they show? How many indexes/databases were demonstrated? Did they show full records? How to save/print/e-mail? How much time, if any, was given for hands-on?

2.5

Observe non-library teachers. Ask if you may sit in for a session or two and watch what goes on. How does a regular teacher greet students? Do the students ask questions? How does the teacher respond?

2.6

Your credibility is very important, or your students will probably not pay attention to what you have to say.

2.7

Inform your audience of your credentials. Even if you are still a library science student, you should have research expertise gained from your undergraduate degree.

2.8

"Expertise, trustworthiness, and goodwill are the primary attributes of credibility. Communicators who are credible have all or at least one of these qualities. There is a complicating factor, however: context."

The size of the audience plays a role in this. "If a prof hopes to gain credibility in a large lecture, he or she must be dynamic and extroverted. These qualities are necessary to capture students' attention.

"Now consider a small seminar. A professor who is bold and talkative, hams it up, and booms out lecture material in a loud voice may be perceived as insensitive or 'in-credible' in a small seminar. In this context, students want a teacher to listen, share information, and help them relate personally to the course. A more empathic, caring style of communication may be perceived as more credible in this situation."[2]

2.9

If you are teaching a small group, you might sit down with them. Standing in front of three students can look silly. If you are demonstrating databases, have the small class sit around one terminal with you. Use a conversational tone of voice in this setting and be sure to give regular eye contact to your audience.

2.10

In front of a large group, make larger, more sweeping gestures. The people in the back of the room need to be able to see them. You are addressing everyone there—not just those in the first ten rows.

2.11

"Just as students must have the will as well as skills to be effective learners, teaching librarians can strengthen their craft through attitude, commitment, and self-knowledge. Consider your educational philosophy and establish that as your standard of classroom excellence."[3]

As you become aware of different learning styles, integrate teaching practices that enhance learning for as many students as is practically possible.

2.12
A good librarian has excellent listening skills. It is important to find out just what your audience needs to learn. Look receptive to questions—it is not enough to ask for them; you must look ready to listen.

2.13
Be alert to raised hands. Call on questioners as soon as possible. This demonstrates a genuine interest in questions and enables you to be sure that your audience understands your current point before you progress to your next one.

2.14
We live in a visual world. Thus, "what people see—not what they hear you say—is what initially occupies their attention."[4]

2.15
Dress and act appropriately or you will lose credibility. It is more important for your students to remember the content of your talk than to remember your clothing.

2.16
If you are younger than most of your audience, you should dress more formally to project credibility.

2.17
"It's better to wear no makeup than to use it badly."[5]

2.18
Unless it is your personal style, do not have your hair, makeup, or clothing stand out. You need to project credibility as a reliable source of information.

2.19
Dress up! It turns out that "people whose appearance suggests high status are treated measurably better than people whose appearance suggests low status."[6] Librarians do not have a reputation for snappy dressing, but you can dress up, not down, for presentations. Feel free to break the stereotype! There is no reason

to have dull attire when you can be creative, within reason. Nevertheless, you do not want your clothes to be more memorable than you are.

2.20
Buying a new wardrobe may not be an option on a small salary (or with graduate school expenses), but consider alternatives for finer clothes—thrift shops, church sales, and hand-me downs from friends and relatives can be useful sources for better clothing. A new-to-you scarf or tie can liven up your outfits with minimal cost. If you must buy new clothing, buy items that coordinate with one another so you can get multiple outfits from one skirt or pair of slacks and so on. Buy classical styles that will last.

2.21
Wear comfortable shoes that you have already broken in. If your feet hurt you will not be able to focus on your audience.

2.22
You will want to feel comfortable when teaching and libraries can be peculiarly heated and cooled. You might need a cozy sweater in summer and wear a short-sleeved T-shirt indoors in winter. Some regions of the country might require a high degree of formality year-round. After you get the job ask about local practice, and once at work, observe the clothing of those around you (not the other new people) to get an idea of appropriate attire. This does not mean you need to sacrifice your individual style, but that you should be conscious of what you are wearing, particularly in front of groups.

2.23
Wear your glasses or get contacts. You must be able to see your sources and your audience. If you cannot see your audience you will lose opportunities to pick up on non-verbal cues of understanding or misunderstanding.

2.24
See Susan Foster, *Smart Packing for Today's Traveler* (Portland, Ore.: Smart Travel Press, 2000) for creative ways to stretch a limited wardrobe over a number of days.

2.25
If you are ill, cancel. Or ask a colleague to substitute for you.

2.26
The exact meaning of a sentence can change depending upon how you emphasize words. Be careful how you give weight to the words you say or your

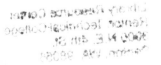

listeners will not be able to differentiate your main points from the rest of your talk.

2.27
Talk directly to the people in the audience. Do not talk to the wall behind them or to the floor beneath your or their feet.

2.28
"Effective communication involves five elements: appearance, facial expression, body language, vocal variety, and information. Studies show that 93 percent of communication is nonverbal."[7]

2.29
Vary your voice when you speak. Change your volume, pitch, and intonation as you talk. Always enunciate as clearly as you can.

2.30
Speak loudly enough to be heard by everyone in the room. Ask if people in the back can hear you. If you have a soft voice, see if you can use a microphone or other sound system. People must be able to hear you!

2.31
If you are speaking in front of a small group, ask everyone to sit near the front so that you do not need to speak loudly. Remember—you are the person with authority—just ask nicely, so your approachability is not jeopardized.

2.32
When working on your public speaking, do not make drastic changes. You do not want to sound artificial. If your class voice and reference desk voice are too different, your perceived sincerity will suffer.

2.33
Speak assertively. Do not sound as if you are uncertain about what you are saying.

2.34
Do not mumble. Be confident!

2.35
Use pauses effectively. Silence is a useful speaking tool.

2.36

If you are a fast talker, slow down.

2.37

Avoid distracting speech patterns: um, ah, you know, er, and so forth. Otherwise audience members might only remember the distractions (and might even amuse themselves counting them) and not the content of your talk.

2.38

Tape yourself talking and listen to it. Then eliminate distracting elements. It is easier to focus on improving one aspect at a time, so consciously eliminate the worst element first, and then work on the others one by one.

2.39

One of the worst speaking characteristics is a monotone voice. Eliminate it immediately if you have one!

2.40

Practice reading aloud to get used to speaking and to practice pronunciation.

2.41

Moving around makes for a more interesting presentation than standing still. Nerve yourself to step away from the primary speaking spot.

2.42

One method of forcing yourself away from one spot is to place one or more of the items you want to show (books, CDs, flash drives, etc.) in another part of the room so that you must walk over to retrieve them. Start small and work up to more frequent movements.

2.43

Using gestures helps you use up nervous energy productively. Also, it is more interesting to watch movement than a still speaker. Meaningful gestures can increase your audience's understanding. For instance, hold your hands far apart when describing large databases and close together for small ones.

2.44

Practice a new gesture to replace one you want to eliminate. Practice it in casual conversation or when you are in front of a mirror. Once it becomes natural, you can add or eliminate another gesture.

2.45
Do not put hands in pockets, do not jingle change or keys, fuss with jewelry, etc.

2.46
If you have a nervous tic or mannerism (you might have to ask a tactful friend what it might be), you will want to eliminate it.

2.47
Before your session, introduce yourself to the group's leader (teacher, professor, principal, CEO, vice president or whomever it might be). Look him or her in the eye when you do this.

2.48
When introducing yourself to the group leader, give a brief but firm handshake. This will project confidence—having this person's trust is important.

2.49
To be credible, you must act and look interested in what you are saying, so avoid a blank or neutral face. Smile and actively look interested.

2.50
"Walk briskly (not too fast or too slowly), stand and sit 'tall,' and you will look and feel more confident. Your voice will repay you by sounding strong and resonant."[8]

2.51
Always face your audience! They need to be able to hear you and you need to be able to gauge their understanding. You need to see when someone has a question.

2.52
It is important to relate to your students—not to interact exclusively to your computer, overheads, or chalk or white board.

2.53
Let students know you have done research yourself. You have been a student and you have turned in papers and received grades.

2.54
Stage fright is a reality for some people. But a most important thing is not to admit to it. Audiences are not as critical as you might think.

2.55
Act as if you are assured and confident. This should help make you feel confident.

2.56
Reduce stage fright with these strategies:
- Prepare, so you know more about your topic than your audience.
- Visit a new classroom more than once before you teach. Stand at the front and become familiar with the locations of light switches, plugs, etc.
- Visualize yourself giving a successful presentation.
- Talk to a few attendees ahead of time so not everyone is a stranger.

2.57
Realize that your audience is concerned about what they will get from your presentation. What they will learn that will be useful to them is much more important than critiquing the presenter. The stakes for you are just not that critical!

2.58
It is essential to adequately prepare for each session or you will have real reasons to be concerned about your presentation!

2.59
Ways to relieve stress:
"Walk up and down stairs . . . Do isometric exercises . . . Breathe deeply . . . Yawn a few times to loosen the jaw . . . Exercise . . . Meditate . . . Visualize."[9]

2.60
Still nervous? Follow a relaxation technique that works for you. For example:
- Take deep breaths and release them slowly.
- Clench your body tightly and gradually relax it.
- Listen to music that calms and soothes you before you teach.
- Try not to schedule meetings right before teaching a session so you can have a chance to pull your performance self together.
- Talk with a friendly colleague whose company relaxes you.
- Do in-office exercises to release nervous energy.
- Surround yourself with calming colors before teaching. Violet (as an accent color) and blue are known to have a calming effect.

2.61
See pages 223-5 in Race, *The Lecturer's Toolkit* for ways to cope with stress.

2.62

Stronge's book (pages 77-88) has useful lists of positive qualities and red flags exhibited by teachers. Red flag examples:
 "Believes that teaching is just a job."
 "Demeans or ridicules students."[10]
The entire book is very helpful, especially for K-12 librarians and teachers.

2.63

"Use different words in each rehearsal to express the same ideas. This will help you keep your presentation 'unrehearsed' and to concentrate on the idea you want to communicate, rather than on the words you are using."[11]

2.64

There is no need to aim for perfection. It will distract you from your main goal of communicating successfully. If you have enough confidence, you will be able to recover from any mistakes. Focus on giving a good presentation, not on the possibility of a mistake.

2.65

When you are teaching your audience needs to know you are interested in their learning, not just in giving your presentation. Listening carefully and responding to their questions and comments is an effective way to demonstrate that you care. (Listening skills are very important at the reference desk as well.)

2.66

Sexism exists: "Men generally are given higher credibility by both men and women—even if the women have better credentials."[12] If you are a woman you will therefore need to more overtly demonstrate your expertise.

2.67

Be available to students for follow up or individual assistance. Also refer students to reference desk.

2.68

Teach at the reference desk: "Watch me do this," or give the keyboard to the user and talk him or her through the search.

2.69

Try to change only one or two mannerisms, voice, speech or other problem with each presentation. Keep wearing the comfortable, ugly shoes, if that is what you need to have the confidence to ferret out "ums" and "ers," walk confidently, etc. Sequence and prioritize needed changes from "urgent" to "would be nice" and take care of the urgent matters first.

2.70

You are not going to please everyone. No one's style pleases every audience. (Is there any celebrity or politician whom everyone, everywhere likes? No. Tastes differ and there will be attendees and group leaders who are not going to like your style.) If you can reach 80% or more of your audiences, figure you are ahead of the game. On the other hand, if you never get compliments, drastic changes are in order.

2.71

Public and corporate librarians will want to keep their talks to trustees and executives to 15-20 minutes. That is the standard presentation time in the business world and you will not want to take more time than expected.

2.72

Consider yourself a recruitment tool for the library profession. By showing your own knowledge and enjoyment of your work, you encourage others to become librarians too.

Notes

1. Edwin G. Ralph, *Motivating Teaching in Higher Education: A Manual for Faculty Development* (Stillwater, Okla.: New Forums Press, 1998), 62.

2. Richard M. Perloff, *The Dynamics of Persuasion: Communication and Attitudes in the 21st Century,* 2nd ed. (Mahwah, N.J.: Lawrence Erlbaum, 2003), 160-2.

3. Abigail Loomis and Deborah Fink, "Meta-Learning: A Transformational Process for Learning and Teaching," in *New Ways of "Learning the Library"—and Beyond: Papers and Sessions Material Presented at the Twenty-third National LOEX Library Instruction Conference Held in Denton, Texas, 5 to 6 May 1995,* ed. Linda Shirato, Elizabeth R. Bucciarelli, and Heidi Mercado (Ann Arbor, Mich.: Pierian Press, 1996), 23.

4. Janet G. Elsea, *The Four-Minute Sell* (New York: Simon and Schuster, 1984), 23.

5. Phyllis Mindell, *A Woman's Guide to the Language of Success: Communicating with Confidence and Power* (Englewood Cliffs, N.J.: Prentice Hall, 1995), 131.

6. Elsea, 33.

7. Karen Kalish, *How to Give a Terrific Presentation.* The WorkSmart Series (New York: Amacon, 1997), 96.

8. Elsea, 50.

9. Kalish, 93.

10. James H. Stronge, *Qualities of Effective Teachers* (Alexandra, Va.: Association for Supervision and Curriculum Development, 2002), 79.

11. Antoni A. Louw, "Break Your Barriers and Be a Better Presenter," ed. Catherine M. Petrini, "Training 101: Stage Fright," *Training & Development,* February 1992: 20 [box in article].

12. Elsea, 28.

3

Customizing Sessions

Before you enter the classroom you need to prepare, so this chapter on customizing sessions is here to help. A sheet of questions to ask instructors seeking a session can be kept by the phone so key concerns can be addressed on the spot (an example is provided).

3.1
Make sure there is a purpose for every session you teach.
- A research paper?
- A speech?
- To make your audience familiar with the layout of the library because they will be using it?
- To learn how to search the catalog?
- To learn how to search specific databases?
- To learn how to search the Web?
- To learn how to differentiate between free and proprietary resources?
- To prepare for a thesis or dissertation?
- To raise money?
- To encourage donations?
- To encourage reading?
- To impress local dignitaries so that they will give funds to the library?
- To promote local programs for the arts/music/sports?

3.2
Never agree to be a time-filler or babysitter! There must be a legitimate reason for the group to be in your library and using your valuable time.

3.3

A question sheet kept near the phone for when library instruction requests are made is useful for newer (and even experienced) librarians, so that all pertinent questions are remembered. Use these questions or formulate your own set. Commentary is so you have reasons for some of your responses. These questions fit on one side of a standard 8½ x 11" sheet. You can also create an online request form, although not all of the questions on the sheet are appropriate for an online form:

Librarian's Question Sheet
(Use when talking with the instructor, or as questions to ask via e-mail)

Instructor's name:_____

Phone #:_____   E-mail:_____

Name of course:_____

Dept.:_____   Level:_____

Date of presentation:_____

Time:_____ to _____

Class location:_____

Meeting class at/in:_____ (classroom, service desk, entrance)

Room Reserved? yes no

1.   Assignment tied to session (ask for a copy, but get details now in case the instructor does not send it or it shows up too late):

»   *If there is not an assignment or other motivation for a student audience, politely decline to give the session. Try not to fill time for an instructor at a conference or "important" meeting.*

2.   Will the assignment be graded? Yes No

3.   What would you estimate as your students' research level? (Some advanced, some novice, all bewildered.)

4.   Will you be attending the session? Yes No If not, will someone else represent you? Teaching assistant or another instructor. *(If the students will be sent unaccompanied, explain why you want the instructor there—mention that you might not be willing to do the session if the instructor is not present.)*

5.   Will you be using time for announcements, handing back homework, etc.? Yes No If yes, how much? _____ minutes

» *If the instructor wants 15 minutes of a 50-minute class, try to avoid giving the session. You cannot do a 50-minute session in 30-35 minutes. You already lose time getting settled.*

6.   Do the students need an introduction to the online catalog? Yes No

7.   Which indexes/databases do you want covered in the session? (Use this as an opportunity to recommend sources—this is why you find out what the assignment is first.)

8.   Which reference sources would you like me to include? (May or may not be something to ask; depends on the assignment. Again, use this as an opportunity to make recommendations.)

9.   Is there anything I need to have special preparation for or to be aware of regarding your students? (Do not offer suggestions here; if there is a special need, the instructor should know what it is. [E.g., student with low vision—larger type size on copy of handouts.])

» *You might now make other suggestions—hands-on exercise, etc. Let the instructor know you are planning this activity.*

Your notes for your preparation for the session:

Materials to hand out/create (e.g., hands-on assignments, if appropriate):

Hold on to this form and attach your handouts; it will be a useful guide for repeat sessions, or as a starting point for related ones.

3.4
Customizing sessions: See if you can get the library session planned into the syllabus when the instructor is writing it.

3.5
Once you have agreed to teach a session, it is time to start preparing for it.

3.6
The best group to teach is one that is on the same page. This is very rare. If you get one or two groups a year with every attendee at nearly the same level of preparation and experience you will be extremely lucky.

3.7

Keep in mind that audiences will have different age groups, backgrounds, experience, and so forth.

3.8

Students will have a much better learning experience if you customize each session. Even though you may be teaching a dozen (or more) sections of the same course, find out the specific interests of each and customize accordingly. A simple sentence in passing that recognizes a class theme will make a noticeable positive connection with the group.

3.9

Aspire to inspire your audience to want to learn even more about doing research.

Assignments

3.10

Negotiate feasibility of assignments with the instructor. Suggest alternatives. Assignments should:
- Have an explicitly stated research objective.
- Define terms.
- Indicate how many sources are required. A minimum with no set maximum is recommended.
- Specify requirements. What types of resources are acceptable? Books? Articles? Web pages?
- Describe the types of resources required. How does the instructor define a scholarly journal article?
- Have students evaluate the sources they use.
- Not require students to use particular index formats (print, CD-ROM, Web).
- Not be scavenger hunts.
- Make research an ongoing process, not just for one project or paper.[1]

3.11

Discuss with the instructor the components of good library-related assignments. There needs to be educational objectives that complement what the students are doing in the rest of their course.

3.12
Do your best to convince the instructor to show up and stay with the session by making it clear that their students will not value or appreciate your instructional efforts without them. Point out that their presence provides opportunities for them to request coverage of additional material and more specific resources. In addition, only the instructor can clarify points related to the assignment(s). If the instructor cannot attend, offer to create a hands-on assignment that students turn into you at the end of the session. The instructor then gives course credit for it.

3.13
Talk through what you plan to do in the class session with the instructor. This is best over the phone or in person. A lot of nuance is lost through e-mail, but it is better than no communication at all.

3.14
Timing of the session is critical. Communicate to the instructor that the presentation will work best after the students have had a chance to think about the assignment. Having had this chance, they will be able to pick up relevant information from you and use hands-on time constructively.

3.15
Get topics from the instructor ahead of time if you can. Students love it when you mention their specific topics.

3.16
Ask for a syllabus. See if there are other projects that you can refer to in your talk.

3.17
Take the initiative on library assignments whenever possible. Patiently and persistently stamp out the "find someone famous with your same last name" assignments. Offer alternatives—someone whose name starts with the same first letter (or starts with the last letter), if the instructor will not budge from the random famous person assignment.

3.18
Research should be an ongoing process, for example:
- The first assignment requires students to search the library catalog for books on specific topics or to identify "known" books or government documents.
- The second assignment asks them to identify articles in indexes found in the library.
- A third asks students to find missing information from article citations known (i.e., personally verified) to be in a specific index relevant to the

course. Then the students find out the library's call numbers (if arranged that way) and locations for the journals and volumes where the specific articles are found.[2]

3.19

Get library research skills into course textbooks when possible. Offer to write these sections and then have the library skills directly relate to the course.

Lecture/Hands-On/Other

3.20

Lectures can be productive way to impart information to a large group relatively quickly. They can be customized for each group.

3.21

Lectures can be problematic if the speaker is weak. In addition, passive students are less likely to be engaged with what is taught and those who have difficulties learning by listening do not benefit from this type of instruction.

3.22

Lectures can work, but students can have short attention spans, so mix it up as much as possible when appropriate. See pages 75-86 of Linda B. Nilson, *Teaching at Its Best: A Research-Based Resource for College Instruction* (Bolton, Mass.: Anker, 1998) on lecturing.

3.23

Recommend to faculty the possibility of tailoring a topic for reliable, free Web resources. If you have time, identify and inform the class of useful resources via a handout or Web page that you create.

3.24

Decide what method(s) you are going to use beforehand:
• 100% lecture
• 50/50 lecture/hands-on
• 10% lecture, 40% demonstration, 30% hands-on, 20% group activity
• Your choice (with input from the instructor)

3.25

Rough out the time you will spend on specific tools:
• 100% online catalog

- 20% online catalog; 40% indexes (specify which ones); 20% hands-on; 20% Web searching.

For example, for a 50-minute session: 10-minute demonstration of online catalog (20%); 5 minutes hands-on (10%); 20-minute demonstration of indexes (40%); 5 minutes hands-on (10%); 10-minute demonstration on how to search the Web (20%). Be sure to allocate within these amounts time for questions.

3.26
Plan the sequence of your sessions. What will you do first? Second? When will students engage in hands-on activities? For how long?

3.27
Bring an outline with you to your presentation. It can have lists of sources you are going to demonstrate and examples that you will search. It may be as detailed or skimpy as you want or need it to be.

3.28
Before you start the session, ask the group leader if the assignment is the same as when you made arrangements. They have been known to change. This gives you an opportunity to design a class while you are literally on your feet!

3.29
If an assignment change would shatter your confidence, call or e-mail the instructor a day or two before the session to make sure that you will not be surprised. That way you will have a chance to revise (or start from scratch) your outline and examples.

3.30
Encourage instructors to give credit for hands-on assignments; this makes knowing basic or advanced library skills a graded and essential part of the course.

3.31
Make sure exercises do not have typos—and if they accidentally do, acknowledge the error as soon as it is discovered and ask students to correct it on their handouts. (We have all had problems at the reference desk looking for the misspelled name of an unfamiliar person!)

3.32
Be aware that the typing speeds in your classroom will vary widely.

3.33

Using media (videos, presentation slides, etc.) for teaching may or may not be practical. If there is no budget to create or buy it, no equipment to run it, or if your classroom is not suited for it, it will not be educationally useful.

3.34

No one method is the best way to teach. Design your session using the best method for a particular learning outcome, taking into consideration the size of the group.

3.35

"The most important [factor] is the number of learners involved. If a maximum of 30 people is to be involved, the investment of time and resources to produce a self-paced multimedia package could not be justified, even though an excellent learning experience might result."[3] On the other hand, if your package will reach hundreds or more for multiple years, it is time well spent.

3.36

Multimedia presentations in a library context must be considered cautiously. Electronic resources have an unfortunate tendency to change in appearance and functionality far too frequently.

3.37

Patricia Senn Breivik lists qualities of good instruction and discusses the effectiveness of various teaching methodologies in her *Planning the Library Instruction Program* (Chicago: American Library Association, 1982). See pages 70 and 72 for an outline of these.

3.38

You can always use more than one method in a given session. You probably have more than one desired outcome too.

3.39

Computer-assisted instruction now includes Web pages and online Web tutorials as means of instructional delivery. Instructional sessions can be conducted (with varying degrees of success) via the telephone, e-mail or virtual reference (asynchronous and synchronous), chat reference (synchronous), bulletin boards, and listservs.

3.40

Self-guided tours can be an effective way to orient people to your library without an ongoing staff commitment beyond checking out the tour (on CD, MP3, or whatever playback technology is currently in favor in your community). Be sure to revise the tour whenever there is a major shift of collections or service points.

3.41
There are many examples of effective teaching strategies in the interesting and thoughtful book *Student Learning in the Information Age* by Patricia Senn Breivik (Phoenix, Ariz.: Oryx Press, 1998).

3.42
Do not plan every word you are going to say in advance. Planning every word is a surefire way to give a dull presentation. In addition, having a fixed text makes it difficult to adapt to an audience that is more advanced (or less experienced) than you expected.

3.43
If you bring 3 x 5" cards as your notes, "punch a hole in the upper left corner. Once you get them organized in the manner you want, bind them together with a large key ring or loop of twine. Then if you drop them, you can easily scoop them up, and they will still be in order."[4]

3.44
Organize your presentation in a meaningful fashion. Group together topics and research concepts.

3.45
Set measurable learning objectives for the students. For example:
A successful student will leave the session knowing how to find the call number and location for a library-owned book when provided with a title or author. This will be demonstrated by successful lookup and call number and location notation of titles provided by the librarian.

3.46
Do not spend too much time preparing for a session. Spontaneity makes a session move better. In addition, unexpected questions will mean you must change your plans. Give yourself time to adapt and adjust your session to the group.

3.47
Leave room for flexibility. Have enough to discuss if there is no audience contribution, but have things you can leave out without missing your main points.

3.48

Bring up topics in current news as examples. They can be local, national, or international, but make sure they are "big" so at least most of your audience will know about them.

3.49

Public library presentations—you are more likely to have a volunteer audience. (Be prepared for the occasional forced audience member—a student required to attend a talk, child of interested parent, or vice versa.)

3.50

"WIIFM Is Not a Radio Station

The whole time you are speaking, the audience will be asking, consciously or unconsciously, 'WIIFM—What's In It For Me?"[5]

3.51

In a library session you can tell students that by the end of the session they will know how to search certain indexes; and if they already have their topics, in a hands-on library lab, they will leave the session with a citation or two.

3.52

Your audience will show up with ideas about how things should be done. Some members will have had either very good or very bad previous library experiences. Everyone has his or her own history that will influence how he or she approaches the session.

3.53

There are learners who will want you to stick with the basic content with no frills. Personal stories and extraneous remarks do not appeal to them. They are in the minority, but do not go so overboard with the jovial approach that you lose entirely those listeners who just want facts—they are there to learn!

3.54

Your "students need to understand throughout these learning experiences how the skills they are learning can be applied to home and work situations. If they finish their education thinking that libraries are only useful for classroom assignments and recreational reading they are not information literate. Indeed, it is this transferability that is the essence of information literacy."[6]

3.55

Focus on the practical. Theoretical library science philosophy is rarely appropriate outside of a library science course.

3.56
A lot of the library instruction literature is far too ambitious. You simply are not going to be able to apply or teach everything offered in the one or two sessions allotted to you. Decide, based on input from the instructor, what the most important things to cover for the session are, and skip the rest. If you are friendly and approachable, students will feel safe asking for additional help at the reference desk or contacting you directly.

3.57
Content is more important than format. The best information may be in—gasp— a book, government document, microform, article, or even on the Web.

3.58
Connect what you are teaching to probable interests and concerns of your audience. Are they going to be completing an ambitious project? Graduating at the end of the year and looking for jobs?

3.59
Not every audience is necessarily going to be students. You may be teaching a special-interest group. For example, trustees whose decision decides funding or sponsorship of programs. What benefits or rewards will they get for supporting the library's goals?

3.60
Pick and choose likely techniques from effective presenters, but only those you can adopt naturally. It is important to be yourself, not a clone of someone else.

3.61
Become aware of your strengths and customize accordingly. Are you a great lecturer? Why not spend more time lecturing? Better at one to one hands-on? Allocate more time for hands-on. The makeup of your audience will be another determining factor in planning. Just make sure that you cover the objectives of each session.

3.62
Develop a set of hands-on exercises that you can quickly adapt to different classes. Have types of searches for your catalog and major indexes/databases ready to be used as is. When you have enough preparation time, put in terms directly related to the session and otherwise customize it.

3.63
Keep up-to-date with the current generation. What are their attitudes toward print and electronic sources? How often do students use Web resources? E-mail?

Chat rooms? A certain number of years ago the class session focused on getting students comfortable enough so they were not worried about the computer blowing up. Now some of them have great computer tips for the librarian. Be willing to learn happily from your learners!

3.64

Keep in mind that the current generation may be older than you are. If your audience is near or past retirement the topics of interest will be different from those who are just starting their adult lives.

3.65

Keep colleagues informed of extraordinary assignments or groups in the library. Let them know the contact name, course number, and course name. (It is astonishing to discover the number of students who do not know even one of these three!)

3.66

When needed, update your examples. Last year's hot topic could be yesterday's news.

3.67

The world is imperfect. If your examples always work smoothly, your students will end up frustrated later when it does not work that way for them. Talk about how you reached the point of having the best (or preferred in the case of subject headings) terms to search.

3.68

Keep a set of folders with handouts and outlines you have created. Have some by topic and others by course. That way when the same topic or course is requested again, you can refer to your earlier notes. What worked? What did not work? Be certain to check your examples to see if they still give the results you expect. Indexes, particularly electronic ones, come and go, and even if they stay, the search results may change.

3.69

Organize your notes on the computer so you can find them when you need them. File names such as "outline" are useless. Give meaningful file names.

Useful Resources

3.70
Association of College and Research Libraries (ACRL). Information Literacy Competency Standards for Higher Education. January 2000. http://www.ala.org/ala/acrl/acrlstandard/standards.pdf

3.71
ACRL Guidelines for Instructional Programs in Academic Libraries. June 2003. http://www.ala.org/ala/acrl/acrlstandards/guidelinesinstruction.htm

3.72
Objectives for Information Literacy Instruction: A Model Statement for Academic Librarians. June 2001. http://www.ala.org/ala/acrl/acrlstandards/objectivesinformation.htm

3.73
American Association of School Librarians. Position Statement on Resource Based Instruction: Role of the School Library Media Specialist in Reading Development. http://www.ala.org/ala/aasl/aaslproftools/positionstatements/aaslpositionstatementresource.htm

3.74
LOEX Clearinghouse for Library Instruction (http://www.emich.edu/public/loex/loex.html) has example materials useful for the librarian preparing for an instructional session. There are links to assignments, teaching sites, tutorials, and more. Their annual conference and conference proceedings from previous years are highly recommended resources for inspiration. If you get a chance to go to a LOEX (or LOEX of the West) conference, take it! Registration is limited to a manageable number of people, so make sure to get your request in early. This is also true of the Canadian Workshop on Instruction in Library Use (WILU)/Atelier annuel sur la formation documentaire (AAFD). WILU/AAFD (English and French) rotates between the east and west parts of Canada. LOEX, LOEX of the West, and WILU/AAFD are great places to exchange ideas and learn new techniques from an exceptionally friendly and helpful group of people.

3.75
An article with a useful overview of library instruction topics, with annotations of useful resources is Maureen Kilcullen's "Teaching Librarians to Teach: Recommendations on What We Need to Know," *Reference Services Review* 26, no. 2 (1998): 7-18. Some of the specifics have changed since this article was published (for example the URL for LOEX [a more recent URL listed above]

and the BI-L discussion listserv is now called ILI-L, sponsored by the Association of College and Research Libraries Instruction Section, and housed by the American Library Association, http://www.ala.org/ala/acrlbucket/is/ilil.htm [accessed May 24, 2004].) But since you know how to do research you will be able to track down current URLs of still-existing services. At least the books and articles will not change their particulars.

3.76
David V. Loertsher and Blandch Woolls, *Information Literacy: A Review of the Literature: A Guide for Practitioners and Researchers*, 2nd ed. (San Jose, Calif.: Hi Willow Research, 2002) is packed with information literacy teaching ideas.

Learner's Search Process

3.77
Six stages of the search process:
"(1) initiating a research assignment; (2) selecting a topic; (3) exploring information; (4) forming a focus; (5) collecting information; and (6) preparing to present."[7]

3.78
Carol C. Kuhthau's six-stage model of search process for advanced high school students and the affiliated feelings is: Initiation/uncertainty; selection/optimism; exploration/confusion, frustration, doubt; formulation/clarity; collection/sense of direction, confidence; preparation (presentation)/relief.[8] See Kuhthau's book, *Seeking Meaning: A Process Approach to Library and Information Services* (Norwood, N.J.: Ablex, 1993) for more details.

3.79
"Bloom's taxonomy of educational objectives . . . the five stages of learning:
- *Knowledge*, or 'the recall of specifics and universals, the recall of methods and processes, or the recall of a pattern, structure, or setting,' e.g., the simple ability to cite information;
- *Comprehension*, or the 'lowest level of understanding,' one in which the 'individual knows what is being communicated and can make use of the material . . . without necessarily relating it to other material,' e.g., the ability to paraphrase or restate information;
- *Application*, or 'the use of abstractions in particular and concrete situation,' e.g., the ability to apply knowledge obtained;
- *Analysis*, or 'the breakdown of a communication into its constituent elements or parts,' e.g., the ability to clarify;

- *Synthesis*, or 'the putting together or elements and parts so as to form a whole,' e.g., the ability to assemble the component pieces in an original manner; and
- *Evaluation*, or the ability to set standards for judgment of information and situations."[9]

3.80
These stages are useful to talk about so students will not feel that they are alone in feeling uncertain or confused.

Team Teaching

3.81
Plan ahead who will be speaking in what order and for how long for each topic. You might decide to go back and forth. Be sure that everyone has seen any handouts beforehand so you all know what is on them.

3.82
Team teaching is recommended for new librarians by Cheryl La Guardia and Christine K. Oka in *Becoming a Library Teacher*, The New Library Series, no. 3 (New York: Neal-Schuman, 2000). See pages 37-9, 41. This book has some good ideas for very nervous new library teachers. It focuses on the practical and reinforces the ideas that disasters happen and it never hurts to practice. The book has a chatty and flippant style, but the scattergun approach does make a few "hits."

3.83
Team teaching works in a number of combinations:
- Two new librarians
- One new, one experienced librarian
- Two experienced librarians
- One librarian, one library staff member
- One librarian, one teaching faculty member
- Three people, in various combinations

The larger the number of students, the more effective team teaching becomes. Do not waste precious staff time on a small seminar.

3.84

After your joint session, talk about what worked and did not work so you can learn from it.

Another Way to Provide Instruction

3.85

A "presentation on PowerPoint that is set up to run in a continuous loop on a personal computer near the entrance to [the] library . . . [shows] a variety of full-color electronic 'slides' informing passers-by about facility hours, recent acquisitions, services, important phone numbers, and other useful information. Removing the keyboard from the computer prevents users from tampering with the slide show. The mouse remains so a viewer may scroll forward or backward through the slides. The timed slide feature in the software allows [viewers] to vary the length of time a slide is displayed in the auto show mode."[10]

Instructional Design

3.86

"Designers who serve as education consultants to other countries [should] become aware of the need to avoid recommending a 'United States solution' to problems in countries where such solutions are ill-suited. This refers not only to media selection, but also to the total instructional approach. Even the translations of instructional materials and rather straightforward directions (as in teachers' guides) must be carefully reviewed to ensure clarity for the user. The importance of this point may be appreciated by recalling that even when designing materials for our own students we are not sure that the communications are understood until they are tested in use by those students. In short, what is perfectly clear to the writer may be very confusing to the reader."[11]

3.87

An excellent book on instructional design is Robert M. Gagné, Leslie J. Briggs, and Walter W. Wager, *Principles of Instructional Design*, 4th ed. (Fort Worth, Tex.: Harcourt Brace Jovanovich, 1992). Read this book if you are interested in instruction and learning processes.

Notes

1. Naomi Lederer, "Designing Effective Research Assignments," Colorado State University Libraries, http://lib.colostate.edu/howto/instr.html (accessed January 23, 2004).
2. Naomi Lederer, "Notes to Instructors on Writing Good Research Assignments," Colorado State University Libraries. http://lib.colostate.edu/howto/instr2.html (accessed January 23, 2004).
3. Patricia Senn Breivik, *Planning the Library Instruction Program* (Chicago: American Library Association, 1982), 68.
4. Lilly Walters, *What to Say When . . . You're Dying on the Platform: A Complete Resource for Speakers, Trainers, and Executives* (New York: McGraw-Hill, 1995), 14.
5. Karen Kalish, *How to Give a Terrific Presentation.* The WorkSmart Series (New York: Amacon, 1997), 55.
6. Gordon E. Gee and Patricia Senn Breivik, "Libraries and Learning," in *Libraries and the Search for Academic Excellence. Proceedings of the Arden House Symposium* (New York, NY; March 15-17, 1987) [See IR 052 055. ERIC ED 284 593], 18-19.
7. Carol Collier Kuhlthau, "Information Skills for an Information Society: A Review of Research. An ERIC Information Analysis Product," ERIC ED 297 740, 1987, 8.
8. Carol C. Kuhlthau, "The Process Approach to Bibliographic Instruction: An Examination of the Search Process in Preparation for Writing the Research Paper," in *Judging the Validity of Information Sources: Teaching Critical Analysis Bibliographic Instruction: Papers and Session Materials Presented at the Eighteenth National LOEX Library Instruction Conference Held at Eastern Michigan University, 11 to 12 May 1990, and Related Resource Materials Gathered by the LOEX Clearinghouse*, ed. Linda Shirato (Ann Arbor, Mich.: Pierian Press, 1991), 9-11.
9. Elizabeth Frick, "Theories of Learning and Their Impact on OPAC Instruction," *Research Strategies* 7, no. 2 (1989): 68-9.
10. Dennis Strasser, "Tips for Good Electronic Presentations," *Online*, January/February 1996: 78- [4 pages]. *Academic Search Premier*, Colorado State University Libraries. http://web8.epnet.com/ (accessed May 12, 2004).
11. Robert M. Gagné, Leslie J. Briggs, and Walter W. Wager, *Principles of Instructional Design*, 4th ed. (Fort Worth, Tex.: Harcourt Brace Jovanovich, 1992), 215.

4

In the Classroom . . . Teaching

A wide variety of students from different backgrounds and different library and life experiences can mean preparing somewhat different presentations if one is going to reach them effectively. The challenge is that these different students often appear in the same classroom, so the target audience is all over the place. Using a variety of teaching techniques in the same session is one way to try to reach your audience. The chapter describes a number of teaching methods (with pros and cons) with practical advice on what to do once in the classroom.

4.1
Show up on time. At least ten to fifteen minutes early to check the room and equipment is best.

4.2
Introduce yourself. What position do you have in the library? Establish your credentials. This increases your credibility. Do not belabor the point, but a brief mention helps. If you are a new librarian you can mention that you have been a student too, and have done research yourself. Experience as a student or librarian establishes you as an expert.

4.3
Reconfirm the specifics of the assignment before class begins. It may have changed since you last talked with the instructor.

4.4

Count out handouts in advance and have them ready to distribute row by row. *See also* chapter 10, handouts.

4.5

"**Don't assume anything**! You can't afford to assume that new students will come to your college all set to make the most of any library they encounter."[1] This applies to basic knowledge of library and research skills.

4.6

You can start your session a number of different ways. Always welcome everyone. Then start with a question, fact, short anecdote, or quotation. Keep beginning remarks brief and relevant to the session.

4.7

Tell them what you are going to tell them.
Tell them.
Tell them what you told them.

4.8

Let everyone know your classroom policies up front. Give reasons for why you are asking them not to do something in your classroom (eat, drink, use cell phones, etc.).

4.9

You might ask where people are from. Just because someone looks foreign it does not mean that he or she is foreign. Ask everyone, so no one person is singled out. This is also a great icebreaker when you know ahead of time (for example, an International English Program class) that you have an audience of foreigners. Asking where the students are from also gives you a chance to gauge their English skills.

4.10

Ask first-year students about the size of the library used most frequently before coming to your library. An audience of non-foreigners can consist of people who have never used a library of your size, so it is foreign to them.

4.11

Do not start with the assumption that your students have used a library similar to yours. They may be used to a smaller, larger, or no library.

4.12
Ask, "Does anyone need to leave early?"

4.13
Start with what people already know and move toward new material.

4.14
Bring an outline with you to the class. It can be very detailed, with multiple typed/word-processed pages filled with examples, or a scrap of paper with scribbled notes (once you have had a lot of teaching experience) of the topics you plan to cover. Refer to the outline as you teach to make sure that you are covering all the topics you meant to cover. Add or subtract items based on student and instructor input.

4.15
Write an outline of what you are going to cover on the board. Add to it based on student comments and questions.

4.16
Ask attendees what they hope to get out of the session. Integrate acceptable goals into your presentation and make arrangements to cover fringe topics at another time.

4.17
Appeal to the common interests of the group. For example, students all have projects due and this session will help them complete them more efficiently and effectively. Or everyone is retiring soon and needs to know what resources are available.

4.18
"If there has been an international or national event of great importance or a local incident that is consuming people's hearts or minds, give them an opportunity to share how they feel or describe what's happened to them. Decide on a time limit. Let them get it off their chest to the whole group or to a neighbour. Refocus and begin again."[2]

4.19
Teaching moment September 11th—Web lines clogged. I was teaching two sections of journalism courses that morning and got to the London *Times* Web site before I could reach U.S. news sites. Sometimes the newer forms of communication may not be reliably accessed. A radio or television station can be accessed (heard) as long as it is still transmitting and you have a receiver with live batteries.

4.20

Acknowledge your students' situations in relation to their assignment. Are they working? Taking other classes? Taking care of family members? Let them know that they need to decide what a manageable topic—that fulfills the assignment—might be.

4.21

Be practical. Most students are not interested in the theory behind your teaching. They just want to get their assignment done.

4.22

Mention where service points in the library can be found.

4.23

If you have a virtual Web tour of your library, show students the link to it.

4.24

Mention the mundane—photocopies cost X, library hours, accessing library databases from home, if available, and so forth.

4.25

Mention nearby resources—other libraries, city offices, organizations, businesses, interlibrary loan (if available), and so forth.

4.26

Mention costs of materials. You do not need to go into specifics, but let your audience know that freely available (to them in the library or through the library Web site) information is not "free."

4.27

Pay attention to your audience, not to your own concerns. If you are well prepared you should have no reason to be self-conscious.

4.28

Constantly watch your audience to see how they are reacting. If you cannot tell if they understand what you have said, ask questions that will elicit useful responses. "Do you understand?" is not as helpful as "Will someone please tell me where I can find the call numbers for books?" A specific question will be a more reliable indicator of understanding.

4.29

Keep the focus on the students by saying "you" often. "You will need to know this for your assignment" is a good reminder to give to students.

4.30

You are not teaching skills in a vacuum. Subject encyclopedias can provide useful background information for other courses. Students will need articles and books for other course projects. A copy of the syllabus will help you identify relevant library resources for more than one assignment.

4.31

Recommend that students do some research before deciding what are the main points (theses) of their papers/projects. This may run contrary to what they are told in class, so call it preliminary research. How can someone know the answer or make a recommendation (thesis statement) before doing any research? If you already know the answer, why do any research at all?

4.32

Mix up your presentation with demonstrations and hands-on assignments. Have students consult with a neighbor when there are class exercises. If you are not in a hands-on classroom, vary the way you give your talk—part demonstration, part lecture, part questions and answers.

4.33

Say the URL as well as writing it. You may have visually impaired students in the room. If there are multiple URLs, put them on a handout to give to the instructor, or have enough copies for the entire group.

4.34

Verbalize all of your actions. "I am now clicking on the 'submit' button." This is especially important in a non- or pre-mouse environment, but it still important when using a mouse. You might even need to elucidate further—I am clicking on the left mouse key. If necessary hold up the mouse (or keyboard) and show just what you mean. You cannot assume that the "enter" or "return" key is obvious. When showing books—"I am looking at the index at the back."

4.35

Use hypothetical examples. Student A tried this, Student B tried that.

4.36

Show/tell alternatives: print, save, e-mail, take notes.

4.37

Have a variety of words or terms at your disposal to describe library topics. For example, library catalog=bibliography=list. Index=list=bibliography.

4.38

"Make it easy for them to remember what you tell them. Give them aide-mémoires such as bookmarks with relevant shelf numbers for their subject area, pens with the university opening hours on or big colourful graphics on the walls to reinforce their learning about the library."[3]

4.39

Mention copyright issues. Define plagiarism.

4.40

Emphasize the function of library materials. It is more important for students to know that there is a resource that does something than to know its name (e.g., organizational directories, specific indexes, etc.).

4.41

What you teach should transfer to other libraries. Your presentation should encompass universal library tenets.

4.42

Do example searches that do not work—not just ones that work. Non-researchers think it is fast and easy for others to find things. Show students that research is not always straightforward.

4.43

Use examples relevant to the class assignment and/or request topics from the group. This works best if the students have had a few days to think about their assignment.

4.44

"Don't be afraid—fear not—to say the same thing—*la même chose*—in different ways to be sure to get your message across."[4]

4.45

Talk about using books effectively. The utility of tables of contents, indexes, and bibliographies is not obvious to everyone. A surprising number of students have never thought about using the index at the back of a book.

4.46

Students will come into your classroom with experience—some of it may even be library experience.

4.47

Emphasize the availability of reference librarians, that students can make individual appointments with you, and the variety of resources available.

4.48

Some interesting ideas are found in John Biggs, *Teaching for Quality Learning at University*, 2nd ed., The Society for Research into Higher Education (Buckingham [England]: Open University Press, 2003).

4.49

"Treat participants' wishes seriously. If you have gone to the trouble of collecting participants' expectations, don't waste them."[5]

4.50

Have students do different tasks when hands-on options are limited by the number of users per database or by the number of terminals available. Ask for feedback on results, ease of use, and utility.

4.51

Suggest practice searches when the stakes are low—no assignment, just explaining the resource/catalog/index, etc.

4.52

Some students may have difficulties using a computer mouse, reading words on the computer, or clicking on objects. It may be related to lack of experience with computers or limited motor abilities.

4.53

Divide different parts of a research task around the classroom. For example, when you have a bibliographic citation showing on the screen, ask different students: Who is the author? What is the title of the article? What is the name of the journal? The volume? The date? The pages? This tends to start slowly and get faster, but is a useful way for students to become familiar with looking for these pieces of information in indexes.

4.54

Debate or discuss issues. Is it better to guess which index to use or ask a librarian? Will you save or waste time by asking? How many indexes are there in the library?

4.55

Look at the group. Body language can be a major indicator of understanding. Do not lecture to an index card, blackboard, or computer screen. Talk to people. They are your audience.

4.56

If your library or a library nearby has assistive technology equipment, mention it from time to time. The equipment may include readers, scanners, printers for Braille, Kurzweil Readers, etc. That way the students with disabilities can learn about these resources without being singled out.

4.57

"Every person in the audience must think you're looking at him or her from a distance of two feet. . . . Half a sentence to a person on the right. A sentence to a person on the left. A thought to a person in the middle, You visit a bit to the right. You visit a bit to the left. A half sentence. A full sentence. A thought. A visit. With practice, your instinct will give you your timing."[6]

4.58

If you are working from a fixed text (at a formal lecture, for instance) you might want to mark up your talk with cues about where, when, and how long you want to pause. However, in the library classroom a fixed text is *never* recommended!

4.59

Encourage students to find more items than required for their assignments. How can someone know that these three articles are the three "best" ones if they are the only ones looked at? Advanced researchers will start seeing patterns—the same expert will be quoted or cited in more than one source.

4.60

Try to include the students as part of a greater research whole. Their contributions and ideas count—but must be well researched to be credible.

4.61

Showing keyboard shortcuts can add interest to a presentation.

4.62

Vary advanced searching tips by audience. All levels probably need to know about Boolean operators. Truncation and proximity operators are useful for a more experienced group.

4.63

Show full index records for articles, books, book chapters, and dissertations. Indicate how students can identify which type of resources is which.

4.64

"Groups of three are easily remembered. . . . If you incorporate alliteration (repeating the same sound at the beginning of the words), retention increases."[7]

4.65

You might ask students to do the short exercises you have prepared in small groups of two or three.

4.66

If you are teaching a session where the class instructor is teaching also, expect to have less time than originally allocated to you, and plan accordingly.

4.67

Move around the classroom. You might need to build up to this, but it helps keep your audience alert.

4.68

Acknowledge problems. Tight library budget? Few new books or journals? Admit it! After all, your audience will need to know that there may be limitations to your collection. This is an opportunity to explain what those tax cuts or stock losses are doing to your collection. Suggest ways to work with what is available by adapting or changing topics, visiting a larger library nearby, using interlibrary loan, and free Web sources. Many assignments can be adapted. Take the initiative and talk with the instructor. If necessary, offer alternatives. "Your students cannot successfully do an assignment on dinosaurs with our library's resources, but we do have an extensive collection of materials on birds."

4.69

Helping students in your office: Have a place for students to sit. If you have a computer, keep it someplace where others can sit by it so they can watch while you search. Or so they can do the searches themselves.

4.70

Do not repeat student answers. It discourages input. Ask the student to repeat the statement. Only repeat to the class if the responder's voice is simply too quiet for the group to hear.

4.71
Do not just give answers. Show how you got to them.

4.72
Do not encourage disruptive interruptions. Find ways to encourage people to wait until you have finished talking. For example, "please wait until I have finished speaking."

4.73
Unfortunately, a group that does not get along with their regular instructor is probably not going to get along with you either. Accept that. Make the best of it, but you cannot expect to change the atmosphere or classroom dynamics in one session. There is no way to know about this in advance; it is something you will realize as your session progresses. Fortunately, this happens rarely.

4.74
There are many variables over which you have no control. Do not let these overcome you when you come across unpleasant ones. You may have to write off (mentally) some sessions, even as you are teaching them.

4.75
Have ways to fill up time when there is an unavoidable delay. Fillers can be useful if there are a few minutes left before a break or if the Internet is particularly slow that day.

4.76
At the conclusion:
• Give a summary of your main points.
• Remind students that reference staff members are there to help them.

4.77
Finish on time.

4.78
After the session, think about what worked, what did not work, and what you might do differently next time. Write down your observations for future reference.

Icebreakers

4.79
Whenever I ask students to work in twos or threes near the beginning of a semester, I encourage them to introduce themselves. However, in a 50-minute session, as a guest speaker, I do not really see my role as the one who gets everyone to feel comfortable with everyone else. That is the regular instructor's job.

4.80
A Bingo game is a way for students to meet one another in the classroom. The idea is from John W. Newstrom and Edward Scannell, *The Big Book of Presentation Games: Wake-Em-Up Tricks, Ice Breakers, & Other Fun Stuff* (New York: McGraw-Hill, 1998). The book has many other ideas that you might want to consider adapting.

Bingo game in library instruction setting (for a longer-than-usual session); you have met some experts in the icebreaker! Students go around room and meet others.

B	I	N	G	O
1st time in library	Wearing something blue	Speaks a foreign language	Keeps Web blog	Has own Web page/site
Checks e-mail more than once a day	Likes Chinese or Mexican food	Has read a magazine at library	Has checked out a book at library	Knows where the restrooms are
Has asked question at reference desk	Wearing shoes with laces today	FREE	Visits a library more than once a month	Reads a foreign language
Reads a newspaper 2+ times a week	Owns a cell phone	Has more than two books checked out	Jogs (more than once a year)	Watches television news 3+ times a week
Has library card	Wears an analog watch	Has more than one e-mail account	Owns more than one dictionary	Has or had a dog or cat

Fill in with your own ideas. Has been in a certain building on your campus or community, eaten in a local restaurant, seen a movie or play at a local theater, has met a local celebrity (mayor, president of university or company), has taken a specific course, plays or played a musical instrument, plays or played a sport (or specific sport(s)), hobbies (knitting, sewing, camping, hiking), color of car, visited foreign country(ies), visited other states (more than 2, more than 5, more than X), has children, grandchildren, etc.

Discussion

4.81
"One of the best ways of starting a discussion is to provide a concrete, common experience through presentation of a demonstration, film or role playing. Following such a presentation it's easy to ask, 'Why did -------?'"[8] For example, ask how many students have written a research paper for another course. Ask about the experience. What would they have liked to have known before they had written it?

4.82
Facts can be looked up. Discussions should establish relationships between ideas of concepts and should be jump-started with factual material.

4.83
Wilbert J. McKeachie has "some concerns about the devil's advocate role. [He] believe[s] that it can be an effective device in getting students to think actively rather than accept passively the instructor's every sentence as 'Truth.' Yet it has its risks, the most important of which is that it may create lack of trust in the instructor. Of course, instructors want students to challenge their ideas, but few want their students to feel that they are untrustworthy, lying about their own beliefs."[9] (Other dangers are discussed.)

4.84
Split the class into talkers and listeners. Discussion will include students in every other row, back/front, left side/right side, etc. That way a dominant talker needs to be silent part of the time.

4.85
Possible topic: Why or when do American and British spellings of words change search results? (Color/colour; honor/honour; behavior/behaviour; organization/organisation.)

Critical Thinking

4.86
Critical thinking is a key component of what you teach! You have found the information—what next? Explain how and why it is important to evaluate resources.

4.87
"To begin, critical thinking requires comprehension. To evaluate reasoning, one must first discover it."[10]

4.88
Students need to be able to distinguish between fact and opinion, and bias is not often explicitly stated. Some students are quite reluctant to challenge the authority of a published source and need to be encouraged to view materials with a critical eye.

4.89
A good critical thinking group assignment is: "Is this a good bibliography?" Hand out a bibliography of resources that supposedly supports a specific topic with:

- A variety of authoritative and suspect resources;
- All authoritative resources; or
- All suspect resources.

Have a class discussion on which, if any, items are relevant to the topic. It is possible to evaluate the worth of a hypothetical research paper.

4.90
Book reviews: discuss inherent bias in publications. Students "need to know that some magazines, journals, and newspapers have a particular ideological, philosophical or political slant." It is important to get more than one review and from different publications.[11]

4.91
Context is also important. Where was the material published? What type of book, journal, or Web page?

4.92
Critical evaluation tools that I use frequently in the classroom (showing the Web page as I do so) are my:

- "How to Evaluate Journal Articles" (http://lib.colostate.edu/howto/evaljrl.html)

- "How to Evaluate a Web Page" (http://lib.colostate.edu/howto/evalweb.html)
- "How to Evaluate a Book" (http://lib.colostate.edu/howto/evalbk.html)

There are some basic similarities between the three evaluation tools. All ask about the purpose, coverage, date, and sponsor of the resource. There are detailed versions of the evaluating articles and Web pages (evaljrl2.html and evalweb2.html). Feel free to use or link to them. The tools are also found in the appendix of my "New Form(at)" article.

4.93
Evaluating means being able to identify underlying assumptions and beliefs. What kinds of proofs are offered to support claims of good or bad? Are parts of the picture being left out? Why?

4.94
"Our proclivity to seek only information that supports our views (called 'confirmation bias' by psychologists), in addition to the human tendency to hold firmly to our beliefs, provide a sizable obstacle to developing the critical thinking abilities of students."[12]

4.95
The "requisite virtues of scholarship in the search for truth include intellectual modesty, openness/teachability, self-awareness, fair-mindedness/justice, coherency and a moderate, reasonable tone."[13]

4.96
See Roland Case, "Making Critical Thinking an Integral Part of Electronic Research," *School Libraries in Canada* 22, no. 4: 13-16, for a good discussion on teaching students to make relative assessments on the reliability of sources, and giving a level of confidence in this assessment.

Tours

4.97
If it has been a while since you have given a tour, do a walk-through before you do your next one. Sometimes a range of books gets shifted, and the animal books are now a few bookcases to the right of where they used to be.

4.98

Try to schedule tours at times of the year that are the least inconvenient. For example, if you are at a university or college, do not give tours during the week before or of finals, or you will be sure to disrupt a large number of students.

4.99

Make sure all or most of the group has gathered near to you before talking about the current location.

4.100

Be sure to welcome everyone to the tour. Ask for their affiliation. What are their interests? What are they studying? This information will help you customize your tour.

4.101

If you have a large group, try to break it into two or more groups—recruit extra staff for a time slot and if small numbers of people show up, take turns leading the groups. Or have a colleague on call for the first five minutes of the tour, so a quick phone call brings another tour leader. Then agree about which itinerary you will each take so you will not trip over one another.

4.102

Depending upon the audience, size may or may not be as major an issue. Highly motivated graduate students will follow and listen attentively in groups of sixty, but for most groups, no more than twenty per tour group is a good rule of thumb.

4.103

Talk in a clear voice. It is better to disturb others in the library for a brief time and move on than to linger whispering and have a large group hanging around near people using the library.

4.104

Encourage staff at service points to acknowledge tour groups and look friendly. This greatly enhances the perceived approachability of your library staff.

4.105

Be conscious of cultural differences. Some groups will stand farther away from you than others. Others will crowd you in a way that might make you uncomfortable, but being aware of different attitudes toward personal space will help you maintain a professional bearing (see chapter 5 for more on cultural differences).

4.106
Try to make the tour a teaching experience if possible. Giving the tour in research strategy order is more useful than just pointing out service and collection points.

4.107
Provide a tour outline to tour leaders. That way each leader can speak in his or her own words, but cover the same topics.

Notes

1.   Sally Brown, Bill Downey, and Phil Race, *500 Tips for Academic Librarians* (London: Library Association Publishing, 1997), 67.
2.   Eleri Sampson, *Creative Business Presentations: Inventive Ideas for Making an Instant Impact* (London: Kogan Page, 2003), 41-2.
3.   Brown et al., 69.
4.   Sampson, 151.
5.   Phil Race and Brenda Smith, *500 Tips for Trainers* (Houston, Tex.: Gulf, 1996), 8.
6.   Hal Persons with Lianne Mercer, *The How-to of Great Speaking: Techniques to Tame Those Butterflies* (Austin, Tex.: Black & Taylor, 1991), 81-2.
7.   Elizabeth Urech, *Speaking Globally: Effective Presentations Across International and Cultural Boundaries* (Dover, N.J.: Kogan Page, 1998), 14.
8.   Wilbert J. McKeachie, *Teaching Tips: A Guidebook for the Beginning College Teacher*, 7th ed. (Lexington, Mass.: D.C. Heath and Co., 1978), 38.
9.   McKeachie, 40.
10.   M. Neil Browne and Kari Freeman, "Distinguishing Features of Critical Thinking Classrooms," *Teaching in Higher Education* 5, no. 3 (2000): 302.
11.   Katherine Dahl, "The Politics of Book Reviews: Or, It's Hard to Say Something Nice When You're Ideologically or Philosophically Indisposed Toward Doing So," in Linda Shirato, ed., *Judging the Validity of Information Sources: Teaching Critical Analysis Bibliographic Instruction.* [LOEX 1990] (Ann Arbor: Pierian Press, 1991), 49.
12.   Browne, 304.
13.   Sonia Bodi, "Scholarship or Propaganda: How Can Librarians Help Undergraduates Tell the Difference?" *Journal of Academic Librarianship,* January 1995: 23. The article gives indicators of both scholarship and propaganda.

5

Diverse Students and Foreign Teachers

A library classroom can include people from all over the planet. Their various backgrounds will influence how they learn and what they expect from their teachers. Sometimes it is the teacher who is on foreign soil. This chapter discusses cultural differences, broadly speaking, from American and other standpoints. There are suggestions both for Americans teaching foreigners (in the U.S. or while abroad) and for foreigners teaching in North America.

5.1
A society's culture is made up of both written and unwritten rules. Some rules are readily apparent, but others are never spoken or otherwise codified. Many times we are not aware of our own cultural tendencies. Within a larger society there are subcultures with their own values. Every family has its own culture. Some "cultures" are temporary—for example, the classroom or audience culture that you will encounter whenever you teach or give a presentation.

5.2
Culture influences people in a variety of ways. Leslie Aguilar and Linda Stokes, *Multicultural Customer Service: Providing Outstanding Service across Cultures,* Business Skills Express Series (N.p.: Irwin Professional, 1996), outline fifty ways on pages 25-6 of their book. Overall areas are etiquette and behavior; beliefs and values; communication; human relations; and time.

5.3
Just because a culture has different behaviors and values does not mean that the people from that culture are behaving wrongly or badly.

5.4

"Because cultures differ in numerous areas such as behaviors, communication styles, functions of language, purposes of human interaction, appropriate roles of teachers and students, and acceptable classroom behaviors, it is not surprising that misunderstandings often occur when individuals from different cultures interact."[1]

5.5

If you are in front of a group that appears hostile or otherwise unreceptive, you might want to acknowledge that you are all in an unfamiliar situation. As an educator it cannot hurt to describe behavioral norms to a newly arrived group of students. Remember, foreign students chose to come to your country so they must make some adjustments to fit in, just like you should when you go abroad.

5.6

"Help gently with acculturation issues. International students can seem very different in their demands and expectations. Some will be really grateful for any thing librarians do to help them, while others will seem to take a great deal for granted. Some students may come from relatively privileged circumstances, and be used to other people doing the running around for them. In these cases, it can take some time for them to attune to the levels of self-reliance expected of them."[2]

5.7

Do not pretend that you are familiar with another culture's values and beliefs. Be open to learning about the other culture.

5.8

"Recognize cultural differences regarding attitudes to alcohol. . . . Class discussions of alcohol marketing strategies or pub social behaviours will be offensive or alien to students (or staff) whose culture forbids alcohol."[3]

5.8

Teaching students from other cultures can make more obvious the problems our own students have with learning.

5.9

Ask the group leader in advance if there are any specific topics that you should avoid. Also, ask what topics the students are interested in. You might have an opportunity to discuss contemporary music or celebrities.

5.10

Patience will be a necessary element when teaching students from another culture. It may take them longer to understand you, so you will need to slow down your pace.

5.11

The library session can be an all-around learning experience. Find tactful ways to describe the social norms at your institution. For example, you could mention that questions are welcome and expected (or not, if that is the case).

5.12

"For students whose first language is a variety of English other than American or British, we must accept that they speak and write fluent English. The problem is not that they are not fluent but that what they speak and write is not our English."[4]

5.13

Be careful not to assume the country of origin of your students. We have a diverse population with second- and later-generation immigrants, as well as people who were adopted as children from other countries. Therefore, it is inappropriate to assume that just because someone looks different his or her language skills or familiarity with American (or British or whatever) culture is limited. If the conversation progresses and a lack of familiarity is identified, additional explanations are going to be more acceptable. Of course, there are native-born and raised citizens who are not familiar with libraries for one reason or another, so the warning about making assumptions applies across the board, not just with "foreigners."

5.14

Ask students whose English is incomprehensible to you to write down their questions or key words. Be especially tactful in a classroom setting, because it may be embarrassing for the student. This is a good practice at the reference desk, too.

5.15

International students often have better reading skills than their understanding of spoken language. Terms may not translate very well either. You will want to have a variety of words or terms to describe library resources.

5.16

Write down key terms on the board (or on paper). At the beginning of your session provide definitions. Partway through, have a quiz to see if the students learned the terms.

5.17
When selecting examples, be aware that international students may not be familiar with local, state, or national concerns. Adjust accordingly.

5.18
If students look uncomfortable when you are looking at them, decrease eye contact for that session.

5.19
If you have hands-on projects for small groups, allow (or even encourage) students who share a language to work together.

5.20
In Australia (and many other Western countries) "success and failure are sheeted back to the students themselves rather than to their teachers. On the other hand, international students may interpret this deliberate shifting of responsibility to students as a sign that the teachers are negligent in their professional duties."[5] By being aware of who your students think is responsible for their learning you can help address their concerns and give you an opportunity to explain the learning expectations at your school.

Generally Speaking

5.21
Even though you might have read about cultural generalities, do not assume that they are universally applied. In addition, the student in your classroom may not conform to his or her society's expectations. Consider the variety of expectations from locally raised students!

5.22
Teaching styles vary from culture to culture. Some cultures demand that students show respect for the teacher at all times, while others accept a more informal approach. Ask students what style they are used to while chatting with them before class. It will give you a chance to learn what they expect from you and will give you a chance to talk about your expectations of them.

5.23
Richard R. Gesteland's *Cross-Cultural Business Behavior: Marketing, Negotiating, Sourcing and Managing Cross Cultures,* 3rd ed. (Copenhagen, Denmark: Copenhagen Business School Press, 2002) has information on specific places for negotiating: on initial contact, relationships orientation, time,

status, verbal communication, paraverbal communication, and nonverbal communication (touch, gaze, gestures).

5.24
"Every human being is surrounded by an invisible envelope of air called a 'space bubble' which varies in size according to (a) where in the world we grew up, and (b) the particular situation."[6]

5.25
There will be times when you are the one who is uncomfortable. Some students may stand closer to you than you like when asking questions after class, while giving a tour, or in your office. Be aware that it may be a cultural difference, but at the same time be willing to inform an individual student (tactfully) that you prefer more of your own space.

5.26
You need to feel safe in your job, and a foreigner (or, for that matter, a local) might impose simply because he or she thinks that he or she can get away with it. There are undesirable people from pretty much everywhere and you should trust your instincts. You might decide to meet with a library user in a public location instead of in your office.

5.27
Some facial expressions need to be used with caution: "the same expression can have a different meaning, sometimes even the opposite meaning in another culture. The same applied to hand and arm gestures. . . . The susceptibility of gestures to misinterpretation reminds us of a universal truth: behavior which is polite and proper in our culture may be rude and offensive in another. . . . *The A-OK Sign*. The thumb-and-forefinger circle is easily the most dangerous and ambiguous of gestures."[7] Recommendation—do not use it. Even if most of your audience looks American, you might have a foreign student for whom it means something quite different than okay.

5.28
"While some interruptions are acceptable in southern Europe and Latin America, conversational overlap is considered ill-mannered in northern Europe, and in the United States."[8]

5.29
"The meaning and use of body posture or stance can vary culturally. In the United States, a culture that values a casual and friendly attitude, people often sprawl when they sit or slouch when they stand. In many more formal European countries, such as Germany, a slouching posture is considered rude. Standing

with hands on hips can be relaxed, bad manners, or a challenge depending on the culture. Sitting with legs crossed may be unacceptable depending on one's gender as well as on the culture with which one is interacting."[9]

5.30

There are useful books on business etiquette by Ann Marie Sabath (two titles: *International Business Etiquette: Latin America: What You Need to Know to Conduct Business Abroad with Charm and Savvy* and *International Business Etiquette: Europe* . . . both Franklin Lakes, N.J., Career Press) that give useful advice, country by country, describing such things as: How dates are written (USA—3/12/80 means March 12, 1980, but in other parts of the world means December 3, 1980); holidays and national celebrations (do not schedule your workshop on one of these); language; religion; business attire; business card etiquette; conversation; gestures and public manners; greetings and introductions; hierarchy; how decisions are made; meeting manners; seating etiquette; when invited to the home; women in business; and lists of things not to do.

5.31

Elizabeth Urech's *Speaking Globally: Effective Presentations Across International and Cultural Boundaries* (Dover, N.H.: Kogan Page, 1998) has numerous speaking tips and gives information country by country on business trends and other information in pages 152-203. Topics covered include attitudes toward time; first names; greetings; dress code; non-verbal communication; what not to talk about (sensitive issues); questions and answers; participation levels; especially for women; and comments. It is a very helpful book.

5.32

Roger E. Axtell, ed., *Do's and Taboos Around the World*, 3rd ed. (New York: Benjamin, 1993) gives advice county by country including do's and taboos on general protocol, names/greetings, punctuality, and conversation. It is a very helpful book.

5.33

CultureGrams (Lindon, Utah: Axiom Press, annual updates) is another excellent resource for information about the inhabitants of various countries around the world, including Canada and the United States. See a map and find information on the land and climate, history, population, language, religion, general attitudes, personal appearance, greetings, gestures, visiting, eating, family, lifestyle, dating and marriage, diet, recreation, arts, holidays, commerce, government, economy, transportation and communication, education, health, and events and trends. This is the most useful and up-to-date resource on country customs (recommended before you travel for leisure, too).

5.34

Find out from your international student office what countries are most frequently represented at your institution and look up information about their customs and cultures before speaking to international groups (or just to know in case they visit the library or the reference desk).

5.35

The most basic advice for Americans is not to chew gum—in most cultures this is considered rude—and not to give chrysanthemums as a host/hostess gift because in many cultures this is a funeral flower.

American Students, Foreign Teacher

5.36

The advice about presenting yourself, eye contact, and interacting with students and instructors described in chapters 2 and 4 applies to all teachers. If there is a suggestion that does not make sense to you, ask an experienced colleague what it means or why it matters to American students.

5.37

Americans are some of the least formal people you will run across in an academic setting.

5.38

If you are a foreigner teaching in the U.S., read the entire book by Ellen Sarkisian, *Teaching American Students* (Cambridge, Mass.: Derek Bok Center for Teaching and Learning, 1997). Highlights are included here, but the book addresses issues beyond the classroom.

5.39

"Do not assume that college students have a common academic background. Unlike educational systems in many parts of the world, American schools have no standard curriculum and there is no single test for the mastery of a shared body of knowledge."[10]

5.40

"American students expect to be recognized, in and out of class as individuals, unique and distinct from their classmates. (This is a cultural value that may be difficult to discern because paradoxically, students also strive to be like their peers.)"[11]

5.41

The conformity in dress and behaviors of students can make it difficult to learn the names of students you see every week. This can be a problem for American-born teachers! One strategy for returning papers to students who look and dress alike (and who also sit next to one another) is to return assignments between them.

5.42

Introduce yourself. Tell students where you come from as a way of sharing that you are foreign.

5.43

Most American students are encouraged to ask questions. Do not discourage questions. Respond to them in a timely fashion.

5.44

American students are not going to be accepting of a teacher whose English they cannot understand. Not comprehending foreign graduate teaching assistants has been a major issue at universities around the United States. You must improve your English language skills if you cannot be understood.

5.45

"Every culture has unstated rules about how close people can stand when they are talking to one another, and under what circumstances people can touch one another. In the United States, for example, you risk misunderstanding by standing too close to someone. The most prudent course is to avoid touching others. If you notice that people back away when you are talking to them, you are probably standing closer than is comfortable in this culture."[12]

5.46

"If you speak with an accent, don't try to change it. And do not apologize for it. Your voice is one of your distinguishing features. Do, however, begin slowly. Very slowly. Your audience requires at least one minute to adjust to your speech pattern. Then if you articulate clearly and project your voice, you will be understood."[13]

5.47

"Ask a colleague for a list of commonly used terms and expressions used in your field. You may also be able to find such terms listed in a glossary or index of an elementary textbook in your field. . . . Ask a native English speaker . . . to record this list onto a tape so that you can practice the correct pronunciation of these terms."[14]

5.48

When teaching, use discourse markers, "words and phrases used to show readers or listeners the relationships between parts of a text or talk. . . .

"*Macro-markers* (longer, more explicit signaling phrases or sentences, see below for example), in particular, are significantly easier to follow than simple transition words (e.g., 'next,' 'for example,' 'so') and lead to increased comprehension. Examples of macro-markers are expressions such as in the following:

"'*You may remember that last time we talked about. . . .*'
"'*What I want to focus on next is another. . . .*'
"'*Let me give you an example to illustrate. . . .*'

"International instructors report that it is also helpful to attend a class of an experienced instructor teaching the same course as you are currently teaching and listen carefully for signaling phrases and sentences. By listening, you will become more aware of their use, and it will be easier to incorporate these helpful signals into your own lessons."[15]

5.49

See Office of Faculty and TA Development, *Teaching in the United States: A Handbook* . . . Ohio State University, Appendix B: Describing Visual Aids and Appendix C: Phrases for Improving Classroom Communication, for several useful suggestions. The entire handbook is recommended reading.

About Americans (for Foreigners)

5.50

Americans like to consider themselves as individuals. Generally speaking, individual goals and aspirations are more important than the well-being of society as a whole.

5.51

In the U.S., "children, boys and girls, are expected to move out, to live alone or with friends, after the basic schooling is completed. This is seen as a sign of independent development: a healthy person not dependent on a group (the family)."[16]

5.52

American women expect to be treated with the same respect given to men.

5.53

There is no one American English. There are regional and even neighborhood differences. It may be difficult for you to understand some Americans' English.

5.54

There are native-born Americans who speak little or no English at all. They will probably not be found in a college classroom, but if you are teaching in a K-12 school or public library it is very likely that you will encounter people who do not understand English.

5.55

To be understood by the largest number of Americans, aim to speak with the non-accented English spoken by well-known newspeople on major (national) television networks.

5.56

If you are going to spend time in the U.S., reading Allyson Stewart-Allen and Lanie Denslow's *Working with Americans: How to Build Profitable Business Relationships* (London: Pearson Education, 2002) is highly recommended. It has explanations about the American mindset (and how it got that way) that would be helpful to the foreigner living and working in the U.S.

5.57

An important thing to remember about Native Americans or the U.S. indigenous population, is that the stereotypical behaviors seen in movies and television are not accurate. Each group (there are over 500 recognized tribes) has its own customs, history, and culture; thus, there is no one all encompassing Native American culture. In addition, individual members of these groups, just like those of any other group worldwide, have their own personal outlook and beliefs.

Fitting In while in the United States

5.58

It is important to show up for appointments on time. If you are going to be late, call ahead and let the person know in advance.

5.59

Introduce yourself to the instructor and to the group you are teaching.

5.60

Give people your complete attention when you are talking with them. It is considered discourteous to be doing something else (e.g., filing your nails) while conversing with others.

5.61
"Americans overall share a willingness to talk about:
- Work
- Sport
- Weather
- Restaurants
- Food, diet, exercise
- Films, theatre, clubs, music."

"Avoid the following topics:
- Politics
- Religion
- Sex . . .
- Sexual orientation
- Age
- Salary . . .
Do not ask about family until family has been mentioned."[17]

5.62
"Do not expect your American colleagues to know what is happening in your area. American newspapers and news programmes carry relatively little foreign news and Americans overall do not pay attention to international business or geopolitical events."[18]

5.63
Shake hands briefly, but firmly in a business/library setting. Look the other person in the eye while you are shaking hands.

5.64
Wine or chocolate used to be the standard gifts when going to an American's home for the first time. These days they might not be as safe as in the recent past. Recovering alcoholics (and those who do not drink alcohol) and people on diets might not truly welcome these gifts. A flowering plant is a good neutral gift unless the household has someone with bad allergies to flowers. With any good luck, you will have a chance to find out if one of these gifts would be appropriate before you are invited to someone's home.

5.65
"One tradition that may surprise a visitor is that of the 'potluck' meal, where guests are asked to bring a main course or another part of the meal."[19] While there may be local variations for this, in more recent years it has become

acceptable to bring purchased food to a potluck. At potlucks, plates, eating utensils, and napkins are usually provided by the host.

15.66
When you are invited to a gathering, it can never hurt to ask the host if you could bring something specific with you. You might be asked to bring ice for the drinks (so American! Ice in drinks—year-round), which can be purchased in bags from grocery and some other types of stores. Ask how many pounds you should bring so you do not buy too much (or too little).

Notes

1. Gayle L. Nelson, "How Cultural Differences Affect Written and Oral Communication: The Case of Peer Response Groups," in *Approaches to Teaching Non-Native English Speakers across the Curriculum*, New Directions for Teaching and Learning, no. 70, eds. David L. Sigsbee, Bruce W. Speck, and Bruce Maylath (San Francisco: Jossey-Bass, 1997), 78.

2. Sally Brown, Bill Downey, and Phil Race, *500 Tips for Academic Librarians* (London: Library Association Publishing, 1997), 79.

3. David Anderson, Sally Brown, and Phil Race, *500 Tips for Further and Continuing Education Lecturers* (London: Kogan Page, 1998), 100.

4. James C. Stalker, "My Language, My Culture: International Variations in Standards for English," in *Approaches to Teaching Non-Native English Speakers across the Curriculum*, New Directions for Teaching and Learning, no. 70, eds. David L. Sigsbee, Bruce W. Speck, and Bruce Maylath (San Francisco: Jossey-Bass, 1997), 14.

5. Brigid Ballard and John Clanchy, *Teaching International Students: A Brief Guide for Lecturers and Supervisors* (Deakin, ACT, Australia: IDP Education Australia, 1997), 19.

6. Richard R. Gesteland's *Cross-Cultural Business Behavior: Marketing, Negotiating, Sourcing and Managing Cross Cultures,* 3rd ed. (Copenhagen, Denmark: Copenhagen Business School Press, 2002), 72.

7. Gesteland, 81.

8. Tracy Novinger, *Intercultural Communication: A Practical Guide* (Austin: University of Texas Press, 2001), 62.

9. Novinger, 67.

10. Ellen Sarkisian, *Teaching American Students: A Guide for International Faculty and Teaching Assistants in Colleges and Universities*, rev. ed. (Cambridge, Mass.: Derek Bok Center for Teaching and Learning, 1997), 17.

11. Sarkisian, 23-4.

12. Sarkisian, 54.

13. Elizabeth Urech, *Speaking Globally: Effective Presentations Across International and Cultural Boundaries* (Dover, N.J.: Kogan Page, 1998), 32.

14. Office of Faculty and TA Development, *Teaching in the United States: A Handbook for International Faculty and TAs 2002* (Ohio State University, 2002), 36.

updated   26   Nov.   2001.   http://ftad.osu.edu/Publications/InternationalHandbook/
PDFChapterlinks.html (accessed May 16, 2004), 37.

15. Office of Faculty and TA Development, 39-40.

16. Allyson Stewart-Allen and Lanie Denslow, *Working with Americans* (London:
Pearson Education, 2002), 98.

17. Stewart-Allen, 219, 222.

18. Stewart-Allen, 224.

19. Stewart-Allen, 248-9.

6

The Classroom

The room where you are teaching can influence your effectiveness. A comfortable environment will enhance the experience for everyone. A poorly designed or uncomfortable space can have a negative impact on learning, and unfamiliar territory can make the presenter feel awkward. This chapter gives suggestions on how to prepare a room for a presentation, and gives recommendations for what to consider when designing a new classroom.

6.1
If at all possible, set up the room the way you like it. Fixed tables cannot be moved, but the placement of movable items is yours to rearrange.

6.2
Check equipment ahead of time with enough lead time to allow for fixes. Nevertheless, always be prepared to cope when equipment breaks down.

6.3
Be a squeaky wheel if there is a recurring problem that needs to be addressed. You should not have to face the same fixable annoyance every time you teach.

6.4
Is there any chalk? Do the markers mark? (Not dry.) Bring some fresh ones with you—after checking that they work. Be courteous and keep markers tightly capped so a colleague is not left high and "dry."

6.5

A personalized welcome sign for your group on the door or next to the classroom is a nice touch.

Figure 6.1 Welcome sign

6.6

I add a reminder about the library lab's food and drink policy.

Figure 6.2 Welcome sign

6.7

A picture that applies to the course theme is a nice touch.

6.8

Have back-up options in case equipment fails.

6.9

"Although you may not be able to control the temperature in any given facility, you could alert participants to bring a sweater or to wear a short-sleeved blouse or shirt depending on the amount of climate control available."[1]

6.10

"Don't have too many chairs. Have only two or three spare chairs; stack up any others in a secluded corner or better still, get them out of the room altogether. Spare chairs often become a no-go zone near the trainer (people sit at the back if there's a back to sit at)."[2]

6.11

If students are going to need to double up in front of computers, inform the instructor in advance so students may be alerted and therefore prepared to share.

6.12

Narrower chairs with wheels as extras are easier to move around than regular chairs. However, since they cannot be stacked they may create a space problem.

6.13

If giving an off-site presentation, go to the room ahead of time and look at it. Where are the plugs (if needed)? How are the chairs arranged? Is there a black/white board with chalk or pens? Where are the light switches? Where will you put down your materials? Stand where you are going to stand and imagine your audience. Test your voice in the room. Is there an echo? A dead sound? Equipment hum? (A/C, lights.) Where are the electric cords? Will you need to avoid tripping over them?

6.14

"Classroom thermostats should keep temperatures between 65°F (18°C) and 68°F (20°C) in winter and between 72°F (22°C) and 74°F (23°C) in summer."[3]

6.15

"Regarding tables, a fixed height of 28.5 inches provides the best surface for multiple uses. It can be use for writing, drawing, computer use, or collaboration. Fixed-height tables are simpler and less expensive than adjustable tables, and always align when nested side by side.

"For dedicated computer use, an adjustable-height table should be considered. Three factors contribute to the need for adjustability: task duration, posture activity level, and availability of an adjustable-height chair."[4]

6.16

From interviews with faculty and students: "The strongest recommendation was to replace plastic tablet chairs with tables and chairs."

Reasons were discomfort and that tablet chairs are "kiddie" chairs.

"Faculty members noted the structure of the tablet chair psychologically isolated students from each other with the tablet providing distance from others. They argued that tables with several chairs automatically created a learning community, small group for discussion, or, at the very least, a place where students belonged with other students." Also the chairs often end up not matching, creating "an unsettling discordant feeling from the lack of aesthetics."[5]

6.17

For usable computer stations, "a clearance of 31 inches above finished floor is needed for wheelchair access . . . 19 inches deep, 36 inches wide, and 32 inches high is recommended" for tables.[6]

6.18

Size of student monitors—if you have a choice, choose for them to be smaller, not larger. You want to see the students. If the classroom has monitors inset into the desks it will not matter as much, but if they are on tables, it will make a difference when you are teaching.

6.19

If the monitors are inset, be aware of the possibility that there might be distracting reflections from the overhead lights or windows.

6.20

Students need room to take notes, and if the monitor and keyboard take up the entire table space they will not be able to do any writing. Hands-on assignments usually involve a place to record results, and there needs to be room for that as well.

School Library/Media Center

6.21

Change the displays in your library media center on a regular basis—the more interesting the better. If they get talked about, great! Involve students in the school in choosing the topic, design, and assembly of the displays. During the topic selection and design stages, use—with the students—your library to find answers and get ideas. Encourage your helpers to bring friends and family to view the results. Then take the opportunity to show the visitors what the media center has to offer. Get helpers from different classrooms in the school to maximize your in-house exposure.

Make sure that it is only the display area that is changed—not the arrangement of your library. A library is challenging enough without the encyclopedias and dictionaries moving around. A favorite author's books need to be on the same shelf for the longest time possible.

6.22
Put resources at child height or your library will not be welcoming or usable.

6.23
Place taller bookcases along the walls so that you have a clear line of sight for as much of the room as possible. Shorter shelving can be placed in the middle of the room.

6.24
Primary school (and public) librarians may find it helpful to use visual clues to sections of the library. Stuffed animals or posters near relevant collections make for a clear section of the room for students to locate desired materials. For example, "The dinosaurs are in the 567.9's under the dinosaur."[7]

6.25
Be sure to have low enough workspaces for your students. A shelving unit that is a good height for an adult to open books upon will be too high for children.

6.26
Write or e-mail organizations and request materials for your media center. See if you can find out from teachers what next year's major topics will be so you can plan ahead. If you have a budget, buy supporting materials. If not, try to suggest that teachers create assignments that use what you do have. Also, consider that the resources may not be at *your* library, but maybe they are at a local public library, or on the Web.

6.27
Become familiar with the holdings of the local public library so you can refer teachers and students to these resources. If there is Web access to the catalog or other materials, provide a direct link from your Web site.

New Classroom/Lab

6.28
If planning a new library lab, try to put it near the reference section, not in a dark corner of the building.

6.29
It is best if classroom seats are not fixed in place.

6.30

An ideal room will have a place for students to hang up their coats, store materials, lean skateboards, and will be close to the reference collection and near the restrooms and drinking fountains.

6.31

An "undersized classroom will be a constant irritation for the instructors as well as the learners. Crowding and the resulting restlessness will not be conducive to learning or teaching. Lack of sufficient space can also lead to violations of accessibility guidelines and fire codes when instructors attempt to 'squeeze in' a few more people. Finally, an undersized classroom may be wasted space and expenditure since, if the classroom is not big enough to accommodate the attendees at an instruction session, that session will be held elsewhere, or—even worse—maybe not at all."[8]

6.32

There needs to be enough space for people to walk behind others and for the items they carry with them to be temporarily stored. Winter coats, backpacks, skateboards, hockey sticks, art portfolios, and/or surfboards might not be common at your institution, but their owners will want to keep them close.

6.33

Size of room considerations are also discussed in Niemeyer, *Hard Facts on Smart Classroom Design,* pages 42-5. The book shows many classroom layouts and includes a useful classroom details checklist (chapter 9, Niemeyer).

6.34

Install as many large white or chalk boards as you can. There can never be too many places to write! In addition, attached boards are better for temporary taping up of materials. Tape can be easily removed from a white board, but may take a bit of the paint or part of the wall itself even when only put up temporarily.

6.35

An open classroom will need a place for lost and found items such as disks or papers.

6.36

An open classroom should have a way to secure valuable equipment. A closet or locking cable will make pilfering attempts more noticeable.

6.37
The teacher's station should have a password if it has access to a projection system, staff drives, or other mechanisms that could be used to be disruptive. In addition, it needs to be immediately available for incoming instructors to prepare for their sessions.

6.38
"Carpet in an electronic classroom must be antistatic and easy to clean so that static electricity and dust do not build up. Carpet tiles may be preferable if cabling is in the floor and carpet removal is occasionally necessitated or if one anticipates areas of heavy wear, (such as the entryway) where it may be desirable to replace the carpet tiles sooner than those in the rest of the room."[9]

6.39
Since opportunities to create new learning spaces occur very rarely, it is essential to carefully consider every aspect possible because you will be living with the results for many years to come.

6.40
When "creating a new classroom, the interests and needs of faculty and students engaged in learning must certainly be taken into account, but also at stake are the interests and needs of the staff scheduling the space, the facilities managers who have a role in the creation of the space, the crew responsible for maintaining the space, the budgeting office responsible for managing supporting funds, even the development office for raising the money in the first place." Other stakeholders are administrators and disabilities professionals (to ensure universal access).[10]

6.41
Make sure that you create a shared vocabulary with the architects as well as other campus departments (facilities, administrators, security, etc.).

6.42
Windows are a welcome addition to any room, but outside windows need to have blinds to block sunlight and reflected light when needed.

6.43
If the classroom will be used by young children be careful to get cords in which they cannot tangle themselves. You might hire a safety expert to ensure that the entire room, including equipment that might be stored or used there, is as child safe as possible. Carts can tip over and televisions and other items can be quite heavy.

6.44

Furniture should be adjustable, comfortable, and sized to fit the tables and the room.

6.45

Carpet on the floor is recommended. It is easier for everyone to hear one another, and softens the sound of footsteps and objects hitting the floor.

6.46

Make sure there is enough space for all the tables and chairs. Students do not want to feel crowded.

6.47

If you can afford more than one classroom, build both a large and a small one. If you have smaller groups it is more productive educationally to have a smaller room so students and teachers are closer together.

6.48

A telephone in the classroom is quite handy.

6.49

Classroom illumination is an important consideration. Have adjustable lighting, depending on the task. See Niemeyer, pages 26-9 on college classrooms.

6.50

Every student needs to be able to see and hear the teacher and see any displays. They need to be able to hear others' voices. Comfort is essential. If chairs are hard and the room is too hot or cold, learning will be sacrificed.

6.51

Conform to the laws for accessibility when designing or reconstructing your classroom (or building). See ADA Law 101-336 (1992). If possible, include in the planning group people with disabilities.

6.52

If you are building a new library or creating a library lab for teaching, *Accessible Libraries on Campus: A Practical Guide for the Creation of Disability-Friendly Libraries* edited by Tom McNulty (Chicago: American Library Association, 1999) is recommended reading.

6.53

For details on classroom design, see Daniel Niemeyer, *Hard Facts on Smart Classroom Design: Ideas, Guidelines, and Layouts* (Lanham, Md.: Scarecrow Press, 2003). This is a great book with specific suggestions.

6.54

If designing an electronic classroom, consult Lisa Janiche Hinchliffe, *Neal-Schuman Electronic Classroom Handbook* (New York: Neal-Schuman, 2001).

6.55

Have clear signs that direct people to the classroom. Include the classroom(s) on building directories.

6.56

Include classrooms on library floorplans and maps. Clearly label them as library labs or classrooms. Show where the classrooms are when giving guided tours.

Notes

1.   Rita Dunn, "Introduction to Learning Styles," in Rita Dunn and Kenneth Dunn, *The Complete Guide to the Learning Styles Inservice System* (Boston: Allyn and Bacon, 1999), 23.
2.   Phil Race and Brenda Smith, *500 Tips for Trainers* (Houston, Tex.: Gulf, 1996), 45.
3.   Daniel Niemeyer, *Hard Facts on Smart Classroom Design: Ideas, Guidelines, and Layouts* (Lanham, Md.: Scarecrow Press, 2003), 36.
4.   Paul Cornell, "The Impact of Changes in Teaching and Learning on Furniture and the Learning Environment," in *The Importance of Physical Space in Creating Supportive Learning Environments* eds. Nancy Van Note Chism and Deborah J. Bickford, New Directions for Teaching and Learning 92 (San Francisco: Jossey-Bass, 2002), 35.
5.   Joan DeGuire North, "Put Your Money Where Your Mouth Is: A Case Study," in *The Importance of Physical Space in Creating Supportive Learning Environments*, eds. Nancy Van Note Chism and Deborah J. Bickford, New Directions for Teaching and Learning 92 (San Francisco: Jossey-Bass, 2002), 75.
6.   Niemeyer, 40.
7.   Mary K. Hobson, "Helping Young Readers Find Their Favorite Book Characters and Subjects," *Library Media Connection*, February 2003, 12.
8.   Lisa Janiche Hinchliffe, *Neal-Schuman Electronic Classroom Handbook* (New York: Neal-Schuman, 2001), 48.
9.   Hinchliffe, 61.
10.   Deborah J. Bickford, "Navigating the White Waters of Collaborative Work in Shaping Learning Environments," in *The Importance of Physical Space in Creating Supportive Learning Environments*, eds. Nancy Van Note Chism and Deborah J.

Bickford, New Directions for Teaching and Learning 92 (San Francisco: Jossey-Bass, 2002), 44, 47.

7

Questions

Questions are an important part of teaching. This chapter talks about handling, encouraging, asking students to respond, and answering questions.

7.1
Ask specific questions. Ask students at the beginning of a session: "What is the assignment?"

7.2
If the assignment has more than one component, try to get responses from as many of the students as possible. This is a speedy way to quickly engage your audience.

7.3
Ask only one question at a time.

7.4
Ask yourself the first question to get things started.

7.5
Be willing to have long silences after your questions. This can be tough, but if you want answers, you need to be willing to wait for them.

7.6
Ask younger students: What grade are they in? What is their favorite subject? What games do they like to play? Ask college students: What are their majors?

What courses are they taking? Where are they from? What library experience do they have? Ask community groups: Are they from the area? Do they visit the library often? Do they have children or other family members who use the library?

7.7
Ask: "What did you learn in your last class session?"

7.8
Listen to students' answers and follow up appropriately.

7.9
Ask and answer your own questions.

7.10
Encourage the instructor to ask questions and otherwise contribute.

7.11
Make sure that your words are understood to avoid confusion. English words can mean many different things. In addition, library terminology overlaps with other fields. For example, abstract paintings or ideas.

7.12
Make sure a previous question has an answer before asking a new one.

7.13
Be sure to acknowledge (not ignore) what students say. The acknowledgment may be verbal or nonverbal, but it should be explicit.

7.14
Ask students to elaborate on short answers.

7.15
More than one student can answer the same question.

7.16
Ask if everyone agrees with a response. Do it in a way that does not challenge the first response or you will have difficulty getting your audience to reply to other questions.

7.17
Ask summary questions. "What are the steps we covered?" Get a different step from different students.

7.18

Try "Quizzing" to review material. Make questions relevant to the topic at hand or relevant generically (such as parts of a complete bibliographic citation).

7.19

Express approval for correct answers. You do not need to go overboard, but most people like praise. Smile when you say "Right answer!"

7.20

Timing of questions depends upon the topic and your comfort level with interruptions:
- Take questions as they come.
- Ask for them to be held to the end.
- Have set times throughout where you ask for them.

7.21

Repeat the question back to make sure you have it.

7.22

Occasionally restate the question in other words. Verify that you have translated it correctly with the questioner before replying to it.

7.23

Folding your arms discourages questions. This is one gesture that is not recommended for use in the classroom.

7.24

Shy audience? Distribute index cards or slips of paper for them to print their questions on.

7.25

Do not belittle the questioner. Be respectful. Look at the person asking the question.

7.26

Give brief answers to hostile questions.

7.27

Call on female and male students. Young and old. Back and front. Left side and right side.

7.28

"Never say, 'I can't *understand* you.' Instead say, 'I'm sorry, I *can't hear* you,' even if you can hear."[1]

7.29

Have students write down questions to give you before class. Group them and answer them in the session. This can be a very effective way to do instruction. Students listen to hear the answer to their questions. You might ask the instructor to ask for questions in advance, so you can group them by research areas.

7.30

"Accept silly questions. When pupils ask 'silly' questions, or say 'silly' things, treat them as perfectly reasonable questions or comments, encouraging other pupils to ask questions or make comments."[2]

7.31

"*What do you do about the 20 percent of the questions that you probably won't anticipate?* If you don't know the answer, say so. Write the question down and tell the questioner you'll have an answer for him or her in a specific length of time (twenty-four hours always has a nice ring to it). By writing the question in plain view of your audience, you demonstrate to the questioner that you *too* think the question is important. If you don't have a detailed answer for the unanticipated question, there's nothing wrong with a short, crisp answer. Most busy people prefer brevity. A 'yes' or 'no' is often more responsive than a reply that drones on forever."[3]

7.32

Direct your answer to the entire group, but start and finish with your eyes on the person who asked the question.

7.33

When teaching about the library there frequently is no cut and dried response. You will often need to say to a student that you recommend that they try more than one resource. Try to list them in order of most likely potential utility. You might want to write down the best resources on your board.

7.34

If your talk is designed for questions at the end instead of throughout, "*Change gear* at the beginning of the Q & A session—by changing your position on the platform, or by perching your bottom on the corner of a table. Say: 'Now let's pause for half a minute, while I get my breath back, and you think about what questions you might want to ask me.'"[4]

7.35
"You aren't the only one who is nervous about talking in front of large groups of people. Inviting questions is important, but the way in which you invite them makes a big difference. You must make the people in the audience feel that it will be safe and comfortable to them to ask questions."[5]

7.36
You might ask the instructor before your session how talkative the group is. That way you can have an idea about the amount of interaction you might have. The same instructor may have a talkative morning class and a silent afternoon section. This happens more often than you might expect.

7.37
"Listen to each question without reaction; then respond simply and directly. If you acknowledge a question as a 'good' question, some listeners may misconstrue your comment to mean that other questions weren't."[6]

7.38
Listen to each question carefully. Filter out possible distracting details such as the questioner's appearance or speaking skills. Look attentive while you listen.

7.39
"When you are working with English (the international business language) with an audience of non-English speakers, you can be straightforward with things like gratitude, praise and enthusiasm.

"Working within your own culture, you often rely on sub-verbal signals to transmit these messages. . . .

"Your international audience is not so well tuned-in to your tone of voice or other implicit message channels. Say it loud and clear:

"What a useful question! Thank you very much!"[7]

7.40
See Bethel's sections on Different Strokes, How Men Can Connect with Women, and How Women Can Connect with Men (pages 152-5) for ideas on communicating with or selling to the other gender (in general). For example, men should be aware of their own stereotypical thinking about women and not act condescendingly toward them; women should avoid acting hesitant and refer less to people, feelings, and relationships.[8]

Notes

1. Lilly Walters, *What to Say When . . . You're Dying on the Platform: A Complete Resource for Speakers, Trainers, and Executives* (New York: McGraw-Hill, 1995), 76.

2. Nick Packard and Phil Race, eds., *2000 Tips for Teachers* (London: Kogan Page, 2000), 47.

3. Ron Hoff, *"I Can See You Naked": A Fearless Guide to Making Great Presentations* (Kansas City: Andrews and McMeel, 1988), 217.

4. Jöns Ehrenborg, and John Mattock, *Powerful Presentations: Simple Ideas for Making a Real Impact*, 2nd ed. (London: Kogan Page, 1997), 93.

5. Antoni A. Louw, "Break Your Barriors and Be a Better Presenter," Catherine M. Petrini, ed. "Training 101: Stage Fright," *Training & Development*, February 1992: 20 [box in article].

6. Karen Kalish, *How to Give a Terrific Presentation,* The WorkSmart Series (New York: Amacon, 1997), 113.

7. Ehrenborg, 94.

8. William Bethel, *10 Steps to Connecting with Your Customers* (Chicago, Ill.: Dartnell Press, 1995), 153-4.

8

Visuals

This chapter talks about using visuals to enhance your presentations. Visuals include black or white board, overhead transparencies, flip charts, and electronic slide shows (presentation software—the most common one being PowerPoint®). Consider using visuals for your presentation only when they are appropriate. They can help people retain what they learn.

8.1
When deciding whether or not to add visuals to your presentation, ask yourself if there is an educational reason for them.

8.2
Visuals are to support your teaching—they should never substitute for content or replace interacting with your audience.

8.3
Visuals need to be effective and efficient. *"Simple and clear . . . visible . . . legible . . . focused and interesting . . . entertaining . . . appropriate and relevant . . . consistent and customized . . . there needs to be a sameness in terms of design[—]uniform colors, graphic style, text, headers (e.g. doesn't look as if random slide from many sources were haphazardly put together)."*[1]

8.4
Just because you have a technology, does not mean that you should use it.

8.5
Talk to your audience. You are not teaching your visual.

8.6
Know when you are going to change visuals.

8.7
Do not have the entire text of your talk on any of your visuals. Instead list key terms, major URLs, and other highly pertinent information.

8.8
The visual is not your script. Do not read it to your audience.

8.9
Keep the visual up long enough for your audience to read it. Stop talking long enough for people to take notes or to think about what the visual says.

8.10
Avoid jargon on your visual unless you are defining it.

8.11
Do not have too many visuals. It is only necessary to highlight key terms and concepts, not every idea you might have to share.

8.12
Advice from a business perspective on presentations: "Never begin or end a speech or presentation with a visual. 'Title' slides should be visible only before the presentation starts so that the audiences will know they're in the right room or can get an idea what the presentation will be about. If you use a title slide, put a blank slide in just after it and click to it before the program begins. This blank stays throughout your opening."[2]

8.13
A closing slide with your name and contact information can be a good thing to leave up at the end of a library session so people can be reminded of your name and know how to reach you later. Or leave your name on the board until most people have left.

8.14
Make sure overheads and computer projections are in focus. Blurry visuals are distracting. Step away from where you are standing, and look at what the audience is seeing. Look at the screen from different parts of the room.

8.15
Only have one idea per chart or graph.

8.16
Use the proper type of chart for the proper idea. In a library instruction setting, the need for any type of chart will be rare.

8.17
"Word pictures can use a variety of graphics (pictures, photographs, clip art, geometric shapes, color key words and numbers, stick figures, silhouettes, line art, underlining, or any symbolic technique) to represent a concept or idea. The key words and phrases are embedded in geometric shapes and linked with lines and arrows to show relationships among the ideas. A line means that some type of relationship or connection exists. Lines can also denote examples of a key idea. Arrows mean cause, product, result, or leads to."[3]

8.18
Bullet points will help keep your visual brief. Full sentences rarely belong on a visual unless part of a quotation.

8.19
"Be sure to make letters big and readable. Presenters shouldn't have to read the visual to the audience; it should be readable from any point in the room. One good rule calls for titles and main headings to be three inches high when projected in an average meeting room."[4]

8.20
"Color brightens a presentation and makes people pay more attention to it. Color can also be used to emphasize a key point. For example, when four lines of blue type are follow by one in brilliant red, the red type fairly screams, 'this is important.'"[5] However, be aware of cultural differences with regard to color and its affiliated connotations. Meanings of colors change as you move around the globe.

8.21
Important (or any) talk? Have someone proofread your transparencies or your slide show.

8.22
Digital camera images can really personalize a presentation. Take a photo of your library, the room you are in, the reference desk, study desks, or computers.

8.23
Corporate librarians: use the company logo/standard template for your presentations.

8.24

Remember, if you are demonstrating an online catalog or electronic index (or showing a book or print journal, for that matter) you are using visuals. In these cases, there is no necessity to create separate visuals.

Black or White Board

8.25

Start with a clean black/white board, or one with only your writing on it. It is your classroom, your board.

8.26

Write on the board with large neat letters.

8.27

Write your name and contact information on the board.

8.28

Go to the back of the room and see if your handwriting on the board can be read.

8.29

Use different colors for different topics. That way you can leave earlier information up with newer content. For example, recommended encyclopedias in green, indexes in black or white.

8.30

Leave your writing up long enough for people to read and write it down. Unless it is somehow distracting, leave it up until the end of the session or until you need the space to write something else.

8.31

There are times when you will invite students to write on the board. One instance would be filling in Venn diagrams.

Overhead Transparencies

8.32

One advantage of overheads is that they can be shared and used for years, as long as the content stays current.

8.33
A second advantage is that it is an older technology that is widely available (the projectors, that is). It is a recommended backup for any off-site presentation you might give. I have been very glad to have them on more than one occasion!

8.34
"If you don't have access to a color printer, use light blue or yellow OHT [overhead transparency] sheets instead of clear which tend to cause glare. Print black on yellow, light green or blue."[6]

8.35
"Remember, any image you create on your computer screen can become an OHT whether it's generated in word processing, drawing/paint, illustration or presentation graphic software. Just put OHT sheets instead of paper in your printer."[7]

8.36
If you have a lot of overheads, take the time to cover with heavy paper or cardboard the unused surface to cut down on excess glare.

8.37
Check your overheads before each presentation to be sure that they are in the correct order and orientation.

8.38
If using presentation software to prepare overheads, be sure to prepare them as overheads, usually with a portrait orientation. Line length will be shorter in this direction, so you will have to consider what you can fit onto the overhead without giving it an awkward appearance—which will happen if you simply change existing presentation slides' orientation from landscape or screen to portrait.

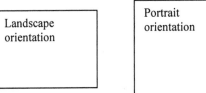

Figure 8.1 Landscape vs. portrait orientation

8.39
Use the cleanest and clearest typeface possible. An overhead is not your opportunity to use an artistic style. If you must show your creativity, do it on an introductory page that does not contain any key information.

8.40

The words on an overhead need to be visible to the entire audience. A day or two before your session, check how your overheads look in the room you will be using them, so you have enough time to redo them if necessary.

8.41

"But type does not by itself guarantee legibility. Simplicity of design and adequate white space are also necessary. Illustrations lifted from texts are almost always too complex for the overhead . . . another element contributing to readability and aesthetics is focus. Your transparency should have focal point where you will place the most important ideas . . . the upper left segment is the area to which the eye travels first."[8]

8.42

It is not necessary to fill up the entire overhead. One brief idea per overhead is best. In many classrooms the lower part of the screen is often difficult for people to see anyway.

8.43

When your overhead starts looking shabby or worn out (text or images start peeling off) throw it away and create a new one.

Presentation Software

8.44

"POWERPOINT SERVES YOU best when it is switched off. People who open PowerPoint software the moment they decide to create a presentation are starting from the wrong place. Planning comes first."[9]

8.45

"The cardinal rule when creating text slides is consistency—consistency when using type fonts and sizes, uppercase text, margins, borders, and color. . . . Use the scheme 'Slide 1 of 35' or something similar to give the audience an idea of the length of the presentation. . . .

"Bullets or other shapes can add interest and emphasis. A wide variety of bullet shapes is often provided with the software, including triangles, check marks, or other variations. Often a bullet that is a different color from the text is eye-catching, just be consistent from slide to slide."[10]

8.46

Only put essential information on your slides. Extraneous texts only adds confusion.

8.47

Overheads/projection software—have plenty of white space! Do not include every word of your presentation. Only include key words.

8.48

Use library themes as backgrounds, or topic-related themes when you know the assignment.

8.49

Customize the background of the slides if you know how. This helps personalize the presentation.

8.50

Ideally have no more than two font styles and sizes per page.

8.51

Use the same font styles throughout your presentation.

8.52

Put in title pages to break up the presentation. This helps introduce the next concept.

8.53

Break up long lists onto as many slides as needed. Indicate at the top of later slides "cont." or the number of the slide (e.g., 2 of 3).

8.54

Have overhead transparency backups for your slide shows. These will need to be reoriented from landscape to portrait orientation. Take the time to make these overheads look good. Proportions are different in this layout, so you will need to adjust your presentation.

8.55

"The most important factor is legibility, which should never be sacrificed merely for the sake of a pleasing color combination. Colors for graphics and text need to contrast sufficiently with the background to be easily read."[11]

8.56

Keep in mind that "colors that are opposite each other on the color wheel—particularly red and green appear to move or vibrate if they are placed sided by side, especially when they're highly saturated. Such color combinations are difficult to look at and should be avoided."[12]

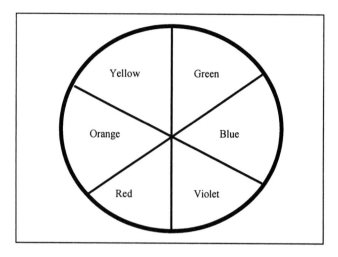

Figure 8.2 Color Wheel

8.57
Depending upon whom you ask, there are different rules for the appropriate number of lines per slide.
7-line rule—this is the one I use.
5-line rule—some instructors swear by this one.

8.58
Fewer lines per slide is always better. The "line rules" are recommended maximums.

8.59
Have a parallel writing style and voice throughout the presentation.

8.60
Use proper capitalization and punctuation.

8.61
I suggest not capitalizing articles and coordinating conjunctions within the title—a, an, the, or, and, but, nor, for—they should be all lowercase unless you have one as the first word. For example, "The Online Catalog," but "Keyword or Subject." Prepositions should also be all lowercase—of, about, with, in.

8.62
Integrate the outline of your talk into the beginning of your presentation.

8.63
If handing out images of your slides, print out black and white versions of them. In some presentation software, this means doing a separate set of slides with dark lettering and light backgrounds. White or yellow letters will print out "blank" slides. Some presentation software has a specific handout printout to use. Unless you are going to use a color printer for every copy, print your master handout in black and white.

8.64
"Vary the layout of your slides every three to five slides, with quotes, questions, charts, tables, symbols, clip art, photos, and/or video."[13]

8.65
"San serif fonts are best suited for electronic presentations . . . some examples of sans serif fonts are Arial, Century Gothic, Eras, Franklin Gothic, Helvetica, Lucida Sans, Tahoma, and Verdana."[14]

8.66
The following slides show proportional arrangements of popular font styles:

Font Style in 72 Point

- Text in 48 point
- Note: 72 points = one inch
- See how much space the type uses
- Alphabet

Figure 8.3 Scaled Example Description

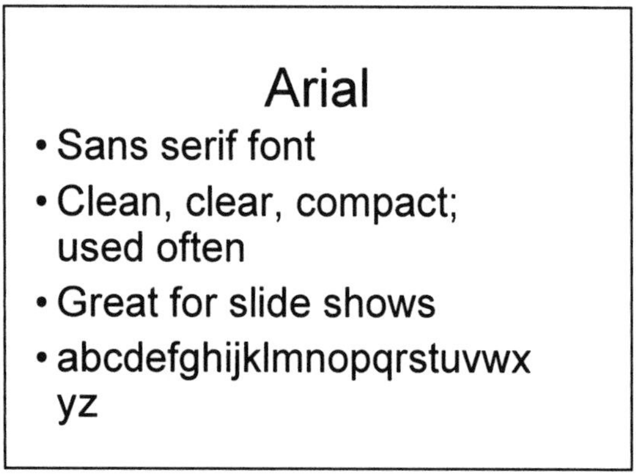

Arial

- Sans serif font
- Clean, clear, compact; used often
- Great for slide shows
- abcdefghijklmnopqrstuvwxyz

Figure 8.4 Arial

Verdana

- Clean sans serif
- Available on most computers
- abcdefghijklmnopqrstuvwxyz

Figure 8.5 Verdana

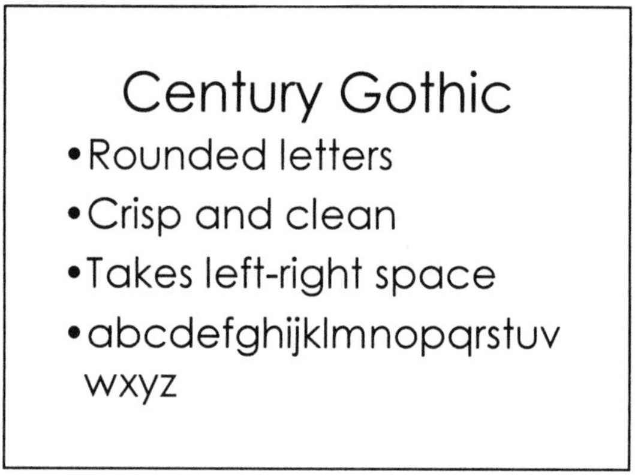

Century Gothic

- Rounded letters
- Crisp and clean
- Takes left-right space
- abcdefghijklmnopqrstuvwxyz

Figure 8.6 Century Gothic

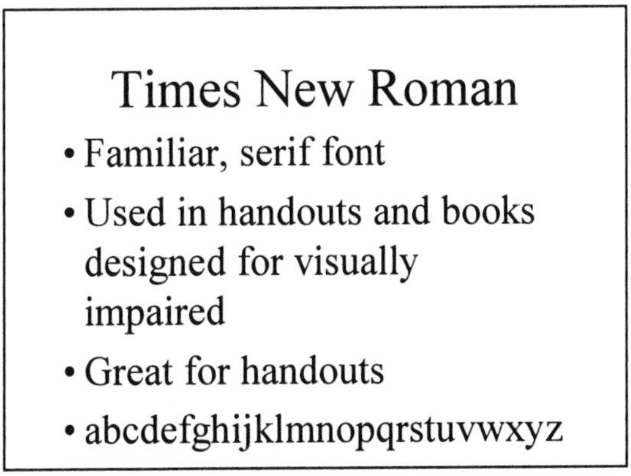

Figure 8.7 Times New Roman

8.67
Pick the best font for the presentation. What appeals to the age group of the audience? Is this to be a serious or playful presentation?

8.68
Scale your images to the proper size outside of the presentation software. Otherwise, the proportions may be off and the image will not be as sharp as it could be.

8.69
Use arrows to point out specific places on slides.

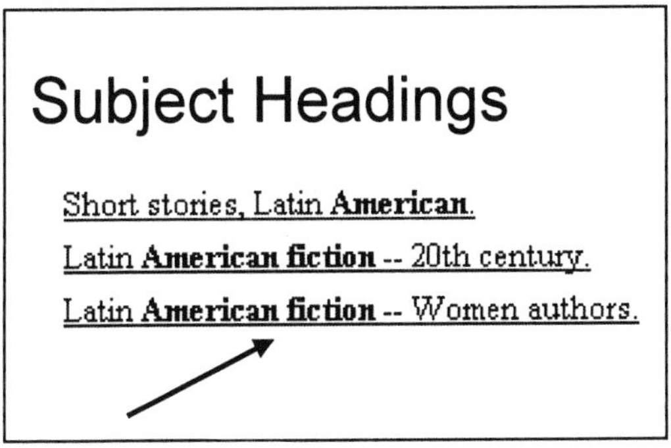

Figure 8.8 Arrow in Use

8.70
Alignment examples below show slides all centered, all left aligned, all right aligned, and all justified.

Centered

Text formatted in the center often
gives the appearance of an overly
elaborate vase. It can be difficult
to read. Centering is for the top
line only.

Figure 8.9 All-Centered Slide

Left Aligned

- Most frequently used for bullet
  points.
- Roman alphabet languages read
  from left to right, so this is the
  easiest format for many to read.

Figure 8.10 All-Left-Aligned Slide

Right Aligned

- Bizarre in English for slides.
- Might be the preferred way for
  languages that read from right to
  left—bullet on right?
- Not recommended.

Figure 8.7 All-Right-Aligned Slide

Justified

- Unless wording just right there are going to be odd spaces on occasional lines.
- Not recommended for any presentation slide show.

Figure 8.7 All-Justified Slide

8.71
"When building your bullets keep in mind Perception Psychology: Audiences find left to right movement natural and easy. Make it easy for your audience. Build your bullets by bringing them in from left to right."[15]

8.72
Displayed below are font styles in 10 point. Notice that some of them are less legible then others. If you want to experiment with a style, ask a colleague or two for input on its legibility. Cute may be unreadable for the visually impaired.

Arial:
ABCDEFGHIJKLMNOPQRSTUVWXYZ
abcdefghijklmnopqrstuvwxyz 1234567890

Century Gothic:
ABCDEFGHIJKLMNOPQRSTUVWXYZ
abcdefghijklmnopqrstuvwxyz 1234567890

Courier New:
ABCDEFGHIJKLMNOPQRSTUVWXYZ
abcdefghijklmnopqrstuvwxyz 1234567890

Garamond:
ABCDEFGHIJKLMNOPQRSTUVWXYZ
abcdefghijklmnopqrstuvwxyz 1234567890

Lucida Sans Unicode:
ABCDEFGHIJKLMNOPQRSTUVWXYZ
abcdefghijklmnopqrstuvwxyz 1234567890

Tahoma:
ABCDEFGHIJKLMNOPQRSTUVWXYZ
abcdefghijklmnopqrstuvwxyz 1234567890

Times New Roman:
ABCDEFGHIJKLMNOPQRSTUVWXYZ
abcdefghijklmnopqrstuvwxyz 1234567890

Verdana:
ABCDEFGHIJKLMNOPQRSTUVWXYZ
abcdefghijklmnopqrstuvwxyz 1234567890

8.73

"Colors often appear different from the monitor display when output to LCD panels, color printers or 35mm slides.

"Because of this element of unpredictability, it bears reminding that after completing your presentation, it is a good idea to take it into a conference room and project it as it will be shown. Check the colors, continuity, and text legibility. This kind of dry run can also help you discover embarrassing typos and other unforeseen problems."[16] Unexpected drawbacks can include poor sound quality in the audio portions of your presentation.

8.74

Take note: PowerPoint has been accused by Edward Tufte (and others) of contributing to simplistic thought and misinformation. Tufte writes that the cognitive style of PowerPoint is "foreshortening of evidence and thought, low spatial resolution, a deeply hierarchical single-path structure as the model for organizing every type of content, breaking up narrative and data into slides and minimal fragments, rapid temporal sequencing of thin information rather than focused spatial analysis, conspicuous decoration and Phluff, a preoccupation with format not content."[17]

8.75

See Edward Tufte, *The Cognitive Style of PowerPoint* (Cheshire, Conn., 2003). He gives a convincing analysis of the problem with the PowerPoint slides that were "directed [to] NASA officials who were making some important decisions during the final flight of the space shuttle Columbia."[18]

8.76 .

Your content is more important than your bells and whistles. Your visuals are to support your presentation, not be a substitute for good pedagogy.

8.77
Use presentation software only when there is a real need for it. It is better to show your online catalog and electronic databases "live" and be a thoughtful speaker. Depend upon presentation software exclusively only when you are in a classroom without a reliable Internet link. Or not at all, by giving a lecture and using other types of visuals such as the chalkboard.

8.78
Now that more conference rooms have Internet connections, I recommend e-mailing yourself any presentation you are about to give. That way if your floppy disk, CD-ROM, or flash drive fails you have another way to get your presentation.

8.79
The more bells and whistles that you have on a presentation, the less likely you will be able to fit it on a floppy disk. If you are not bringing your own equipment to a remote site, make sure that the site's computer will accommodate a CD-ROM or flash drive.

8.80
Presentation software can be a lifesaver when your classroom Internet connection fails. If you have an unreliable connection, create presentations that you can use when live searches are not an option. Make them resource-based, so you can selected the exact topic you need. For example, create separate shows that demonstrate your online catalog, frequently used indexes, full text database(s), and so forth.

Flip Charts

8.81
Large groups will not be able to see a flip chart. They are best for small groups.

8.82
"Dark blue and black pens work best for text and bright blue, green and red for accents and diagrams. Yellow, brown and orange don't show up well."[19]

8.83
Test colors in the room you will be using. Certain wall colors may absorb or otherwise make some colors difficult to read.

8.84
Invest in pens that do not bleed through the paper.

8.85

The bigger the room, the thicker the marking pen or chalk, the larger the letters.

8.86

Flip chart advantages:

- They do not break down (unless you run out of paper or ink—so plan ahead).
- Changes are easy—you can start on a new page if your current page gets too messy.

8.87

If you prepare pages in advance, write as neatly as possible or ask a colleague with good printing to make them. Quality expectations are higher for materials prepared in advance.

8.88

As with other visuals, only write down key terms and phrases on your flip charts.

8.89

"If you will need to refer back to a previous flip chart, attach a large paper clip or binder clip to that page to make it easier to find."[20]

8.90

"Pre-cut several pieces of masking tape and stick them to the flip chart easel. It will make it faster when you need to hang your sheets. Use tape that won't damage the wall surfaces."[21]

8.91

If you know what you are going to write down ahead of time, prepare those pages in advance of your session.

8.92

Invest in a stable easel for the flip chart. If an easel is constantly on the verge of tipping over it be will a distraction (and could hurt somebody). You will want to feel comfortable writing.

Videos

8.93
Watch any video you might show ahead of time. First to decide whether or not to use it, and secondly to know the content and be ready to answer questions about it. On class day, cue up the video to be sure it is the one you mean to show.[22]

8.94
Stay in the room and watch with the students. If you leave you are suggesting that the content is not worth watching.

8.95
Follow up the video viewing. Make time for discussion and questions. Relate the video to the rest of the session.[23]

8.96
Have a handout summarizing the video clip, and be ready to talk about key points from the video excerpt in case the video does not work.

8.97
"Capture your best presentations. When you know you've polished a presentation to a fine art, make a video of it. You can then use the video as a training session tool, and additionally be there as 'expert witness' to address questions arising from the content of the video. This can also give you a chance to recover your voice during an extended training session!"[24] If your library has the equipment to tape an often repeated session, you can offer it as an alternative to a library session when your lab is booked or no one is available at the time the class meets.

Notes

1. Ray Anthony, *Talking to the Top: Executive's Guide to Career-Making Presentations* (Englewood Cliffs, N.J.: Prentice Hall, 1995), 224-5.

2. Karen Kalish, *How to Give a Terrific Presentation.* The WorkSmart Series (New York: Amacon, 1997), 68.

3. Thomas C. Cyrs, "Visual Thinking: Let Them See What You Are Saying," in *Teaching and Learning at a Distance: What it Takes to Effectively Design, Deliver and Evaluate Programs,* New Directions for Teaching and Learning 71, ed. Thomas C. Cyrs (San Francisco: Jossey-Bass, 1997), 30.

4. Virginia Johnson, "Picture-Perfect Presentations," *Training & Development Journal,* May 1989: 46.

5. Johnson, 46.

6. Dona Z. Meilach, "Overhead Transparencies Designed to Communicate," *Arts & Activities,* May 1992: 43.

7. Meilach, 50.

8. Cyndy Gribas and Lynn Sykes, "Creating Great Overheads with Computers," *College Teaching* 44, no. 2 (1996): 66- [3 pages]. *Academic Search Premier,* Colorado State University Libraries. http://web8.epnet.com/ (accessed May 12, 2004).

9. David Tebbutt, "Presentations Made Perfect," *Director*, October 2003: 46.

10. Dennis Strasser, "Tips for Good Electronic Presentations," *Online,* January/February 1996: 78- [4 pages]. *Academic Search Premier,* Colorado State University Libraries. http://web8.epnet.com/ (accessed May 12, 2004).

11. Jon Hanke, "The Psychology of Presentation Visuals," *Presentations,* May 1988: 42-51. *ABI/Inform,* Colorado State University Libraries. http://jake.prod.oclc.org:3055/ (accessed July 9, 1998).

12. Hanke.

13. Jennifer Rotondo and Mike Rotondo Jr., *Presentation Skills for Managers* (New York: McGraw-Hill Briefcase Book, 2002), 49.

14. Rotondo, 55.

15. Jerry Weissman, *Presenting to Win: The Art of Telling Your Story* (Upper Saddle River, N.J.: Financial Times Prentice Hall, 2003), 130.

16. Strasser.

17. Edward Tufte, *The Cognitive Style of PowerPoint* (Cheshire, Conn., 2003), 4.

18. Tufte, 7.

19. Eleri Sampson, *Creative Business Presentations: Inventive Ideas for Making an Instant Impact* (London: Kogan Page, 2003), 72.

20. Barry Weissman, "Training Low-Tech Style," *Industrial Safety & Hygiene News,* November 2002: 31.

21. B. Weissman, 31.

22. David R. Torrence, "Training with Television," *Performance & Instruction* 33, no. 3 (1994): 27.

23. Torrence, 29.

24. Phil Race and Brenda Smith, *500 Tips for Trainers* (Houston, Tex.: Gulf, 1996), 77.

9

Using Web Pages

Web pages are extremely useful resources in the library classroom. Not only are materials owned by many libraries now identifiable via Web catalogs, but there are electronic indexes and content databases. If your library has its own site, you can create Web resources specifically tailored to your instruction (or reference desk) needs. I constantly use them in the library lab, and they can be great 24/7 resources for your students. Researchers can get librarian recommended terms to search in the catalog or find out which indexes to use at 3 a.m., should they choose, and the librarian does not need to be awakened to give the research advice. The library without walls is here; embrace its utility.

9.1
Develop your own Web site. This is especially helpful for a repeat course or very subject-specific topics. The old-fashioned annotated bibliography placed on the Web is still a very useful and used resource.

9.2
Once you have a research outline that works, it can be quick and easy to create other Web pages on similar topics. Just be sure to replace all the specific terms that would give away the history of the page!

9.3
Use a Web page during a session:
- "to outline and guide the presentation,
- to present examples,
- to expose students to resources and provide links to digital information in specific subject fields, and

- to provide an enduring class resource after the session is over."[1]

9.4
Students can use the Web page later to review what they learned in class.

9.5
Some other librarian or scholar may already have a Web page on your topic. Point it out and use it. The Web makes it possible to use resources found in other locations. Take advantage of these freely accessible sources.

9.6
An annotated Web page is much more useful than a list, but if time is tight, a linked list is better than nothing. During your class session you can annotate verbally.

9.7
A Web page can substitute for a class session. Offer to create a Web page for faculty members and get their input on what you create. For an example of this type of page see:
"Stylistics" http://lib.colostate.edu/research/english/stylistics.html

9.8
You can save your Web pages to disc or CD-ROM and thereby be able to show them in classrooms that do not have a live Internet hookup.

9.9
You can use the Web to reach a wide audience—for a description of what I did at Colorado State University see "New Form(at): Using the Web to Teach Research and Critical Thinking Skills," *Reference Services Review* 28, no. 2 (2000): 130-53. Note: parts of the site have been dismantled, the main "How to Do Library Research" has changed since the article was published (new instruction program), the first-year composition program is now handled differently, as mentioned in the introduction, and now there is a group creating instruction pages and tutorials. However, most of the pages can be found via one of my subject pages or through a Web search engine. The Language Research Topics described in the article are accessible via the English Language & Literature page and the Speech 200 pages are found via the Speech page.

9.10
The way students use the Web is different than one might expect. They tend to go directly to URLs, not through the menus that have been carefully laid out. See my article, listed above, for an analysis to the hits to the pages that demonstrate that there was no way that students were using the site as I

expected—pages that were layers down had more hits than the pages above them. Some of the pages are being identified via Web searchers or as direct links from others' pages. "How to Evaluate a Web Page" is my most recent "best seller," but the "Double Talk, Euphemisms, and Professional Jargon" has continued to have a strong showing. Other popular pages include: "Popular vs. Trade vs. Scholarly Journals," "Library of Congress Subject Headings," and "Venn Diagrams." Popular subject pages include "Policy Topics Research—Example Speeches," "Finding Literary Criticism in Articles," "Finding Literary Criticism in Books," "Elizabethan/Stuart," and "Stylistics." And the numbers overall are much, much greater than the hits reported in the article. The site is seeing more use all of the time.

9.11
Create Web pages in languages relevant to your audience. If you do not have a staff member with the skills, it is worthwhile to pay someone to translate the key pages on your site. You may need to spend time with the translator explaining library jargon and vocabulary. The translated pages will be appreciated and used. For a description of a bilingual site as an outreach tool, see Awilda Reyes and Naomi Lederer, "Bilingual Outreach: 'Research for Teens' on an Academic Web Site," *The Reference Librarian* 82 (2003): 141-55.

9.12
A Web site can reach your audience campus, city, state, nation, and worldwide to anyone with Web access. You can teach without leaving your building.

9.13
Point to items on the Web in languages that your audience reads. For example: "Comment évaluer des articles de journaux" (http://lib.colostate.edu/howto/french/frevaljrl.html) and "Cómo evaluar artículos de periódicos" (http://lib.colostate.edu/howto/spanish/spevaljrl.html).

9.14
Talk about privacy issues concerning the Web. K-12 and even older populations should not be putting personal information about themselves on the Web. See Naomi Lederer, "Alert! There is a Lack of Privacy on the Web," *Academic Exchange Quarterly*, Fall 2000: 74-5, for a discussion of this topic.

9.15
Color contrast on Web pages is important because otherwise your audience will have difficulty reading them.

9.16
Keep URLs short (as short as you possibly can).

9.17
Royalty-free images can be found on the Web. Search .gov sites and check individual pictures closely for copyright statements. You can also purchase royalty-free images (see examples of these in use on "Research for Teens," http://lib.colostate.edu/teen_research/).

9.18
Web colors do not all look identical on PCs and Macs. Stay with the basics.

9.19
Before redesigning your Web site, visit "Web sites of university libraries located around the country. This is one of the key advantages for anyone involved in a major Web redesign project. With little effort and no impact on the libraries' travel budget . . . see what [your] colleagues around the United States have done to organize access to library materials through the Web and the type of instruction offered by each library though its Web."[2] Visit sites from other countries while you are at it, too.

9.20
User accessibility is very important The following is an excerpt only:
1. *"Provide equivalent alternative to auditory and visual content.* Provide a text equivalent for every nontext element, including images, graphical representations of text, image-map regions, animations, applets, ASCII art, frames, scripts, sounds audio files, and video. . . .
2. *Don't rely on color alone.* Ensure that text and graphics are understandable when viewed without color. Approximately 5 percent of Web users experience some degree of color blindness. . . .
3. *Use markup and style sheets, and do so properly. . . .*
4. *Clarify natural language usage.* Use markup that facilitates pronunciation or interpretation of abbreviated or foreign text. . . .
5. *Create tables that transform gracefully. . . .*
6. *Ensure that pages featuring new technologies transform gracefully. . . .*
7. *Ensure user control of time-sensitive content-changes.* Some disabilities prevent users from reading moving or scrolling text. Make sure these can be paused or stopped.
8. *Ensure direct accessibility of embedded user interfaces. . . .*
9. *Design for device-independence.* Users should be able to interact with their preferred input device, whether it is by mouse, voice, keyboard, etc.
10. *Use interim solutions.* Some older assistive technologies and browsers do not interpret page elements correctly. Some elements that cause difficulties are pop-up windows, tables, forms, and adjacent links. Until these can be handled by newer technologies, consider avoiding their use or provide alternative versions.

11. *Use W3C technologies and guidelines. . . .*
12. *Provide context and orientation information.* Group different page elements and provide contextual information. . . . Be certain to title each frame to help users navigate.
13. *Provide clear navigation mechanisms.* Navigation should be clear and consistent. Incorporate sites maps and tables of contents. Make text links meaningful.
14. *Ensure that documents are clear and simple.*"[3]

9.21
During the design of a new Web site (or to find out if your existing site is user-friendly), the "best results come from testing no more than 5 users and running as many small tests as you can afford."[4] Test with five, redesign, test with another five, redesign, and test again with five new users.

9.22
"You need to test additional users when a website has **several highly distinct groups of users**." Jakob Nielsen recommends:
- "3-4 users from each category if testing two groups of users
- 3 users from each category if testing three or more groups of users (you always want at least 3 users ensure that you have covered the diversity of behavior within the group)"[5]

9.23
See additional practical advice on user testing (and the more detailed explanations found in the article), linked to from Jakob Nielsen's article, "Why You Only Need to Test with 5 Users" on http://www.useit.com/alertbox/20000319.htm

9.24
Test your Web site in more than one browser.

9.25
Doctor HTML, http://www2.imagiware.com/RxHTML/ can be purchased to do an electronic Web page analysis. It reports any problems it finds. As of May 2005, cost for a site license was $350. Multiple servers require multiple licenses. See the Web site for details.

9.26
Bobby will check Web pages for accessibility compliance for Web Content in two ways; either Accessibility Guidelines 1.0 or U.S. Section 508 Guidelines. URL: http://bobby.watchfire.com/bobby/html/en/index.jsp

9.27

Additional topics and resources for evaluating a new or revised Web site can be found on "Research-Based Web Design & Usability Guidelines," sponsored by the National Cancer Institute: http://www.usability.gov/guidelines/index.html

9.28

A viewer should not have to scroll down on your main page.

9.29

Have descriptive labels ("alt text") for your images and avoid distracting and potentially epileptic triggering blinking images and text. Your audience needs easy-to-read information.

9.30

Identify authors and site owners whenever possible. There is educational fair use, but avoid copyright infringements.

9.31

Update your Web pages whenever needed. If you cannot keep a page up-to-date, remove it.

9.32

Try to write as many timeless pages as possible. Specific database ownership may change, but research strategies do not.

9.33

Offer to create subject specific pages for your teachers or faculty. Coauthorship is another possibility.

9.34

A software that automatically checks URLs is an extremely useful tool. Get one for your library if you can. There are free and fee versions.

9.35

Like any other educational tool, keep your user in mind when creating online instruction pages and tutorials.

9.36

"Online instruction solves several problems. Online modules can be used at the student's convenience. Because the modules can be delivered over the Web, they are accessible from remote locations. Online instruction also provides an alternative for students who prefer self-regulated learning rather than formal instruction, and it allows for the possibility of self-paced exercises. Interactive teaching methods, incorporating sound, graphics, text, and demonstrations are more effective for those students who gain little benefit from oral presentations by a librarian or instructor."[6]

9.37
If you are interested in creating Web tutorials, Susan Sharpless Smith, *Web-Based Instruction: A Guide for Libraries* (Chicago: American Library Association, 2001) is highly recommended. It covers the gamut of topics needed to create Web pages, including technical information about mark-up, etc., and has an extensive list of resources.

9.38
Font size and size of images may be impacted by the size of users' monitors and modem speeds (the latter becoming less of an issue as time progresses, but still must be considered).

9.39
Basically, "appropriate design is the act of matching the demographics and content of your Web site to specifically chosen colors, shapes and type styles. This ensures that the combination of visual elements adds up to a design that's suitable to the content, and fits the audience with no need for additional tailoring."[7]

9.40
"Color choice is paramount in eliciting an appropriate visual response from visitors. Color is one of the first things your audience sees, and you can set up your pages so that color appears immediately. . . . If you're representing a community Web site, for example, you'll typically want to choose warm colors to create a sense of comfort and ease. If your site is meant to be informative, with the words carrying most of the weight, the site colors should be simple and not distracting . . . choose colors that reflect your audience's values."[8]

9.41
Simple is better than elaborate. For example, Web pages that use Java script can create annoyances for the people who want to print.

9.42
Library Web pages reach a wide audience and you do not want to make your site difficult or confusing to use. Not every user has the latest equipment or DSL line.

9.43
Web pages are a good way to promote your library and its services. They are
outreach tools. Make them as user friendly as you can.

Notes

1. Ralph Alberico and Elizabeth A. Dupuis, "The World Wide Web as an
Instructional Medium," in *New Ways of "Learning the Library"—and Beyond: Papers
and Sessions Material Presented at the Twenty-third National LOEX Library Instruction
Conference Held in Denton, Texas, 5 to 6 May 1995*, eds. Linda Shirato, Elizabeth R.
Bucciarelli, and Heidi Mercado (Ann Arbor, Mich.: Pierian Press, 1996), 30.
2. Anne M. Patoff, "Redesigning the Library Web Site: Implications for
Instructions," in *Library User Education in the New Millennium: Blending Tradition,
Trends, and Innovation: Papers Presented at the Twenty-seventh National LOEX Library
Instruction Conference Held in Houston, Texas, 11 to 13 March 1999*, eds. Julia K. Nims
and Ann Andres (Ann Arbor, Mich.: Pierian Press, 2001), 116.
3. Susan Sharpless Smith, *Web-Based Instruction: A Guide for Libraries*
(Chicago: American Library Association, 2001), 92-4.
4. Jakob Nielsen, "Why You Only Need to Test with 5 Users,"
http://www.useit.com/alertbox/20000319.htm (accessed September 20, 2003).
5. Nielsen.
6. Mary Ann Tricarico, Susan von Daum Tholl, and Elena O'Malley, "Interactive
Online Instruction for Library Research: The Small Academic Library Experience,"
Journal of Academic Librarianship 27, no. 3 (2001): 220.
7. Molly E. Holzschlag, "Satisfying Customers with Color, Shape, and Type,"
New   Architect: Internet   Strategies   for   Technology   Leaders
http://www.webtechniques.com/archives/1999/11desi/ (accessed May 16, 2004).
8. Holzschlag.

10

Handouts

Handouts are the most basic of visual aids. They give your audience something to hold on to and take with them to consult after a session. This chapter gives suggestions for what to include and how to design your classroom and other handouts.

10.1
"Lectures and classroom discussion are often improved by the use of simple handouts in advance of or at the beginning of a class. Particularly effective are graphs, charts, data sheets, cartoons, photos, sketches, diagrams, and maps—may of which (depending on copyright laws) you can simply photocopy and distribute to your class."[1]

10.2
Do not inundate your audience with paper.

10.3
Give a detailed handout to the instructor.

10.4
Include your name, phone number, and e-mail, URLs, key terms, key databases. There is no need for details.

10.5
Half sheets or even quarter sheets work just fine. (And are more cost-effective for tight budgets.)

10.6
Do not go too small with type sizes. The smallest useful size for handouts is 10 points.

10.7
Do not use an inappropriate font style. But have fun if you can. Use the same style throughout. A light-hearted style can brighten your audience's day.

10.8
Use different-colored paper if you have multiple handouts and are going to refer to them (or have students do hands-on). Be sure to have different headers or titles on them for those who cannot tell the difference between colors.

10.9
Only use light-colored paper for handouts. Purple might be a fun color to you, but it is extremely difficult to read text on it.

10.10
Stiffer paper is recommended for bookmark-sized handouts.

10.11
Topics for small-sized library handouts include:
- Library hours
- Library URLs
- Library phone numbers
- E-mail or virtual reference information
- Location information

10.12
Clearly delineate different sections of your handouts with larger sized headings and bold type.

10.13
"Use white space. For students to develop a sense of ownership of handouts, they need to have room to write their own notes on them."[2]

10.14
Handouts are useful for hands-on activities. Ask for call numbers and locations of books, complete bibliographic citations, numbers of items found on a specific topic (keyword vs. subject search), format of specific years of journals (bound volume, microform, electronic). Include space on the handout for student responses.

10.15
When creating group exercises, leave enough room for everyone's name and their responses on the sheet you hand out. If you assign roles, have the roles listed so that the participants can indicate which part they played. For example: recorder, keyboard, spokesperson.

10.16
Keep electronic copies of your handouts so you may update them quickly. Print only enough for each session.

10.17
If your library has a drive accessible to all staff, put handouts designed for courses taught by multiple librarians on it. That way there can be a uniformity of content for the course instruction, and each librarian teaching them can put his or her own name on it. You can also attach the file to an e-mail message.

10.18
See Interrogating Your Handouts, table 3.1 in Phil Race, *500 Tips on Group Learning* (London: Kogan Page, 2000), pages 113-5, to see what elements to look for in your handouts.

10.19
Make sure you own handouts follow a consistent bibliographic style. Use a recognizable, relevant style to the topic at hand. For example, use APA for psychology courses, MLA for English literature, and CBE for engineering.

10.20
Put the file location, name, and date on your copy of handouts. Not on a computer? Still put a date on it.

10.21
Give files sensible names—course number or topic. "Outline" is meaningless the moment you have a second one.

10.22
When preparing a handout in Braille, do not center headers or anything else. Keep them on the appropriate side (left for English—punched out "backwards" from the right side).

10.23
Consider the size of your font in handouts. The "official" size for the visually impaired is 14 point. Use it on handouts for this audience. Have an option for creating a copy in an even larger size, on request.

10.24
"Handouts provide the most efficient and cost-effective means of transmitting large amounts of factual information. There is no reason why patrons should have to write down information on library hours or circulation rules during an orientation session. . . .

"All handouts of a single library should be compatible in style and format. Guidelines in these areas should be developed and carefully followed. . . . Handouts should be dated and the chief author should be indicated."[3]

10.25
For an example of a library publication policy, see Naomi Lederer, "Library Publications Policy: Guidelines for Publications Displayed in the Arizona State University Libraries," 1992. ERIC document ED 357 757.

10.26
Bibliographies should be arranged in a meaningful research strategy sequence. Divide resources by type (encyclopedias, indexes, etc.) or location. However, do not divide resources by format within type. Keep indexes with indexes and indicate the format next to the citation.

10.27
"Handouts can be given to learners in advance of, at the time of, or following the lecture. Prospective distribution allows the audience to read preparatory material or to ponder particular questions. Dispensing with background information, the lecturer can subsequently cover more subject matter or begin at a higher level. If the advance handout contains questions, the classroom session may be more interactive. However, antecedent handouts often go unread.

"More commonly, handouts are provided at the beginning of a class, providing a 'program guide' for the lecture. While this allows key points to be highlighted and eases the strain of note-taking, concurrent distribution encourages two types of inattention. Convinced that whatever is worth remembering has been transcribed, part of the audience may daydream, while others shuffle through pages, attending more to the handout than the speaker."[4]

10.28
Class handouts can be in a wide variety of formats and content. Lists of key resources (including preferred subject terms) are always useful and save students from having to write down what you are telling them. You can also create

interactive handouts where students fill in the information as you relay it during class.

10.29

Print out or make enough copies for everyone. Keep an extra copy or two for your folder so you can refer to it the next time you teach that class.

10.30

"Avoid underlining a word that has been highlighted with the use of capital letters; this kind of emphasis adds a difficulty to the decoding of that word or phrase."[5]

10.31

"Like all-capital printing, the excessive use of italics and bold variants slows reading of continuous text. Use italics or bold only to emphasize and highlight small amounts of text embedded in sentences and paragraphs, or to make headings stand out. . . .

"Use italics and bold for highlighting important material, not underlining. Underlining may cause visual interference with letters, distracting the reader or exacerbating the letter discrimination difficulties. For example, . . . 'y' as 'v' or 'u.'"[6]

10.32

"In addition to providing more perceptual clues for letter recognition, proportional type allows you to use a larger point size without requiring more space on the page."[7]

- `Example of monospaced type (Courier New).`
- Example of proportional type (Times New Roman).

10.33

Make sure your handouts have a balanced look. Margins need to be wide enough for readers to hold the paper and to take notes.

10.34

A library handout should not be a densely filled page of text. An outline format will be the most appropriate format in most cases.

10.35

Use familiar typefaces.

10.36

Design. There are four basic principles:

"Contrast . . .
"If the elements (type, color, size line thickness, shape, space, etc.) are not the *same*, then make them **very different.**
"Repetition
"Repeat visual elements of the design throughout the piece. You can repeat colors, shapes, textures, spatial relationships, line thickness, fonts, sizes, graphic concepts, etc. . . .
"Alignment
"Nothing should be placed on the page arbitrarily. Every element should have some visual connection with another element on the page. . . .
"Proximity
"Items relating to each other should be grouped close together."[8]

10.37
Flyers that you put on bulletin boards are handouts too. They need to be designed to be legible and informative.

10.38
Include the who, what, when, where, and why on your flyers. Be specific about dates, times, and places. Think about your audience. Remove flyers immediately after the event.

10.39
The flyer you design for faculty will be different from the one you design for students. If you can, ask one or two members of your intended audience for feedback before printing and distributing them.

10.40
Do not put too much information on a flyer. Present the needed details as clearly as possible and stop. Pique interest without telling all. Main topics should be enough.

10.41
"Before you sit down to design the brochure, fold a piece of paper into the intended shape and make notes on each flap. Pretend you just found it—in what order do you read the panels?
    "Keep in mind the order in which the panels of a brochure are presented to the reader as they open it. . . .
    "The fold measurements are not the same on the front as they are on the back! After you fold your paper sample, measure from left to right on front and back. **Do not simply divide 11 inches into thirds**—it won't work.
    "It's important to be aware of the folds; you don't want important information disappearing into the creases!"[9]

10.42

Are you creating flyers and brochures? Read all of Robin Williams, *The Non-Designer's Design Book: Design and Typographic Principles for the Visual Novice* 2nd ed. (Berkeley, Calif.: Peachpit Press, 2004), which is a rather fun book with lots of examples that show just what she is talking about with regard to designing documents.

10.43

"Optimum type sizes vary dramatically for children as they grow older, and grow more proficient in the mechanics of reading. In the earliest stages, when they are striving to recognize individual characters or groups of characters, sizes as large as 24pt are used. But as the child's reading skills advance, so the need to recognise word shapes (rather than their constituent letters) becomes more important so smaller type is preferred. By the age of 12, the preferred size-range is much the same as an adult's.

"Attempts to establish an optimal size of type for adults with normal eyesight have been made, but an optimal size is difficult to determine because the question is so closely related to tracking, kerning and leading. . . . However, reliable investigations show that the common type sizes (given as 9 to 12 point) are of equal readability, whilst 10pt is the 'preferred' size. As sizes increase above 12pt, reading becomes progressively slower for the same reason that larger sizes are helpful to younger children—the word shape takes second place to individual characters."[10]

Hands-On Assignments

10.44

When student have chosen their topics before coming to a library instruction session, hands-on time can be spent searching for resources on their topics. Free search time is generally wasted, so if students do not have topics give them a worksheet to fill out.

10.45

Be sure to leave enough space for students to write their responses. Blanks need to be long enough to fit numbers of items found (or bibliographic information) and people's writing is larger than you might expect. Younger students will need longer lines and wider spaces to have enough room for their answers.

10.46

Start with basic questions and then raise the level of expected knowledge for later questions. For example (this example does not have enough room for student answers; much more space is needed for most of these, especially numbers 4 and 7; you might want to double space numbers 5 and 6 as well as making longer lines):

Using the online catalog, write down the number of items the library owns for questions 1-3. Answer the other questions as asked.

1. Word search: journalism _____ items
2. Subject search: journalism _____ items
3. Author search: Graham, Katherine _____ items
4. Title search: *Do the Media Govern?: Politicians, Voters, and Reporters in America*? Who is the editor?
5. Fill in the following information for the book whose title begins: *Hello, He Lied*.
   a. author _____
   b. complete title _____
   c. city of publication _____
   d. publisher _____
   e. date _____
   f. call number _____
   g. location _____
6. Give the following information for a book written by Walter Cronkite:
   a. complete title _____
   b. city of publication _____
   c. publisher _____
   d. date _____
   e. call number _____
   f. location _____
7. Give the complete citation, call number and location for a book which has "journalism—objectivity" as a subject:

10.47

Notice how the questions evolve from "type this in here and give a number" to presuming that the student not only knows which kind of search to use, but also knows the parts of a citation. You can create a similar progression for an index (printed or electronic).

10.48

Include images of buttons or search screens from online sources as part of the hands-on assignment (and be careful to update these images as needed).

10.49

Put file locations and names on hands-on assignments (in small size—well, one that you can still read, anyway) so you can find them on your computer to

update. At the top have a space for students to put their names (Name: _____);
this not only gives ownership of the document, but is important when you have
convinced the instructor to give credit for doing the assignment. Offer to provide
an answer sheet to the instructor. You will have to update this the next time you
use the assignment. Moreover, I have seen different, correct numbers of items
depending upon the time of day when students completed an assignment.
Sometimes a catalog or database gets updated in the middle of the day. Let the
person grading the assignment know this so students do not get marked wrong
for what was a correct answer.

Notes

1.   Alan Brinkley et al., *The Chicago Handbook for Teachers: A Practical Guide
to the College Classroom* (Chicago: University of Chicago Press, 1999), 7.
2.   Phil Race, *500 Tips on Group Learning* (London: Kogan Page, 2000), 112.
3.   Patricia Senn Breivik, *Planning the Library Instruction Program* (Chicago:
American Library Association, 1982), 76.
4.   Kurt Kroenke, "Handouts: Making the Lecture Portable," *Medical Teacher* 13,
no. 3 (1991): 199- [5 pages]. *Academic Search Premier*, Colorado State University
Libraries. http://web8.epnet.com/ (accessed May 8, 2004).
5.   Arthur Hoener, Spencer Salend, and Sandra I. Kay, "Creating Readable
Handouts, Worksheets, Overheads, Tests, Review Materials, Study Guides, and
Homework Assignments Through Effective Typographic Design," *Teaching Exceptional
Children,* January/February 1997: 33.
6.   Hoener, 34.
7.   Hoener, 34.
8.   Robin Williams, *The Non-Designer's Design Book: Design and Typographic
Principles for the Visual Novice,* 2nd ed. (Berkeley, Calif.: Peachpit Press, 2004), 13.
9.   Williams, 105.
10. Zara Emerson, ed., *About Face: Reviving the Rules of Typography* (Mies,
Switzerland: RotoVision, 2002), 74.

11

Humor

Humor can be a touchy topic in the classroom. Some people think it is inappropriate. However, it has its pedagogical uses, so there is no need to shy away from humor if you are naturally amusing.

11.1
Never force yourself to use humor. It you cannot be funny naturally, do not try to make yourself be amusing. It will not work and you will come off as lame.

11.2
Humor should be used judiciously. Too much of it in a classroom setting may distract from your main points.

11.3
You do not want to insult your audience. You want humor to be a shared positive experience.

11.4
Humor does brighten up a class session. It perks people up and lightens the load of learning.

11.5
"One of the most important functions of humor is to create a positive learning environment. Laughter in the classroom is a sign that students are enjoying learning instead of resisting it as a dull effort demanded of them by adults."[1]

11.6

"When teachers show they have a sense of humor and aren't afraid to use it, students relax and become listeners. In this respect laughter can represent a certain amount of freedom from the constraints of the classroom. . . . However, humor is not a replacement for repetition as a teaching methodology. And humor has been shown to be most effective when the jokes and anecdotes which supplement a particular lecture are related to the material being taught."[2]

11.7

"Jokes have the greatest impact when they are delivered with brevity. . . .

"Ideally, it is best to set up your joke with a series of no more than two or three bits of information followed by a punchline."[3]

11.8

Jokes should probably be used sparingly in the library classroom. No more than two per session is recommended and they need to relate to the topic at hand.

11.9

Humor has its uses in the classroom. "In some instances, in fact, it can help form a cultural bond between teacher and pupils. Over time, a teacher and a class might build up an understanding coded partly in humour. After a certain episode, a simple signal may spark off its recall, with full humorous effect."[4]

11.10

It is possible to integrate a spontaneously humorous remark or incident as a theme of a one-time library instructional session. It cannot be forced, but if it happens by itself, take advantage of the opportunity and weave the humorous theme into the rest of the session. For example, if a search results in a humorous book title, look up the same topic in the next index you demonstrate.

11.11

"When students are asked to identify characteristics that describe exemplary teachers, one of the first descriptors offered is, invariably, a sense of humor."[5]

11.12

A sense of humor is a way to lighten the time waiting for slow computers and downed databases.

11.13

By using humor you are showing your audience that you enjoy your subject—libraries and research. Enjoyment and enthusiasm can be shared and can serve as a good substitute for more traditional forms of humor. In general, people who show that they enjoy what they are doing are more effective than those who are just doing a job.

11.14
Exaggeration in your voice is a form of humor. "Come on, come on!" you can urge a slow computer.

11.15
Humor in the classroom should be upbeat, not negative. Give a cheerful view of reality, not a grim one.

11.16
When it comes to humor, it "is not:
- Taking more time to plan your lessons
- Becoming a stand-up comedian
- Drastically changing the way you're doing things in your classroom"[6]

11.17
Humor livens up a classroom and does not interfere with learning. It promotes learning. Class is more fun for everyone when humor is included.

11.18
Anything that elicits a smile or laugh counts as humor! It need not be something that fits into traditional humor. You can be humorous without telling funny stories or jokes.

11.19
"There are teachers who are very concerned with getting a specific amount of information covered by the end of class. Many refuse to even recognize an appropriate humorous occurrence or comment. But when something funny happens students are going to laugh, with or without the teacher's permission. Sometimes, when appropriate, it may do more good just to stop for 10 seconds, recognize it and continue rather than ignore it and have students snicker and giggle for the rest of the period."[7]

11.20
Humorous bits are often the most remembered. Try to get in key points near (but not at) the time of laughter.

11.21
If you are fortunate enough to have a student or two who make comments on the lighter side, enjoy them! The humor does not have to come from you to brighten the moment.

11.22

Ask while waiting for a slow computer (or for groups to return from other parts of the building, etc.) if anyone has any fun stories to share.

11.23

Keep in mind: "Certain cultures may not recognize humor as socially acceptable; and, also, at various times in a person's life humorous situations may not be appreciated."[8]

11.24

If there has been some grim event locally or nationally, humor will probably not be appreciated in the days immediately following the event.

11.25

Low-risk humor:

"(1) quotations and questions, (2) cartoons, (3) multiple-choice items, (4) top 10 lists, (5) anecdotes, (6) skits/dramatizations, and (7) ad-libs that aren't." For example, if the projector light goes out, "I knew I should have used the low-tech chalkboard."[9]

11.26

"Don't use ethnic or off-color jokes. Keep your jokes clean, nondiscriminating, and kind. Don't use self-deprecating humor or humor that belittles your competence (people in the audience will subconsciously wonder why they are listening to you). Don't use humor that belittles someone else's competence."[10]

11.27

Inappropriate targets of humor "to avoid at all times: (1) put-downs of any individual, including a popular entertainment, or political personality; (2) put-downs of any group based on ethnicity, race, gender, religion, or sexual orientation; (3) sarcasm and ridicule; (4) sexual content and innuendo; (5) profanity and vulgarity; (6) humor about physical disabilities and characteristics (e.g. fat, short, blond, pregnant) and mental handicaps; and (7) humor about extremely sensitive issues (e.g. AIDS, abortion, divorce, personal tragedies)."[11]

11.28

"As every teacher knows, each group creates its own chemistry. One class of students is gregarious and responsive to humor, while another is sleepy, bored or hostile. A group's sense of humor depends on many factors including physical comfort, interest in the subject matter, the attitude of the teacher, and the time of day."[12]

11.29

Light amusement works well across cultures, but jokes do not tend to travel very well.

11.30

Do not use humor in any way that suggests that you might be incompetent. You will lose the respect of your audience if you seem not to know what you are doing.

11.31

Just being very cheerful is a form of humor. You do not need to be traditionally amusing.

11.32

Show cartoons that relate to libraries. Explain why or why not the way libraries are presented is accurate. This is an excellent critical-thinking exercise.

11.33

Look up topics that are humorous themselves or result in humorous results (you will need to prepare for the latter in advance). I often use the title *Hello, He Lied*. It is good for a giggle. Assemble your own list of titles.

11.34

Sometimes homographs bring up some bizarre (not even remotely close to the topic you were looking up in a keyword search) results. These can lighten the moment too. "Why did *this* article come up? Oh—the word is the author's last name!"

11.35

See a number of twisted expressions, one-liners, and quotations on pages 24-7 of Berk's book *Professors Are from Mars®, Students Are from Snickers®* (Sterling, Va.: Stylus, 2003).

11.36

For a bibliography of humor books and journal articles with ideas both offensive and inoffensive see pages 53-9 of Berk.

11.37

An excellent selection of one liners (and just funny painful happenings) is found in Lilly Walter's book.

Notes

1.   Deborah J. Hill, *Humor in the Classroom: A Handbook for Teachers (and Other Entertainers!)* (Springfield, Ill.: Charles C. Thomas, 1988), 20.

2.   Hill, 21.

3.   Hill, 76.

4.   Peter Woods, "Coping at School through Humor," *British Journal of Sociology of Education* 4, no. 2 (1983): 113.

5.   Judy P. Pollak and Paul D. Freda, "Humor, Learning, and Socialization in Middle Level Classrooms," *Clearing House,* March/April 1997: 176- [3 pages]. *Academic Search Premier*, Colorado State University Libraries. http://web8.epnet.com/ (accessed May 8, 2004).

6.   Jerry King, "Laughter and Lesson Plans," *Techniques: Making Education and Career Connections,* January 1999: 34- [2 pages]. *Academic Search Premier*, Colorado State University Libraries. http://web8.epnet.com/ (accessed May 8, 2004).

7.   King.

8.   Gayle Webb White, "Teachers' Report of How They Used Humor with Students Perceived Use of Such Humor," *Education* 122, no. 2 (2001): 338.

9.   Ronald A. Berk, *Professors are from Mars®, Students Are from Snickers®: How to Write and Deliver Humor in the Classroom and in Professional Presentations* (Sterling, Va.: Stylus, 2003), 23, 44.

10.   Karen Kalish, *How to Give a Terrific Presentation.* The WorkSmart Series. (New York: Amacom, 1997), 31.

11.   Berk, 45.

12.   Hill, 46.

12

Learning Styles, Different Learners

People are different, so it should be no surprise that they learn in a variety of ways. Using assorted teaching methods helps reach the largest number of students. Knowing some of the different ways people learn should help you better adapt your teaching to your audience.

12.1
Try to accommodate as many learning styles as possible. Tell, show, and if possible, have attendees do hands-on activities (the latter works best if students already have their topics chosen or if the librarian provides specific things to search).

12.2
Have a variety of ways that you teach a topic.

12.3
You cannot generalize learning. Just because someone is older, younger, or majoring in a certain subject, does not mean that they learn in a specific way.

12.4
A positive learning experience includes different ways of presenting the materials. Some students learn best by listening, others by seeing, and others by doing.

12.5
No matter what the learning style, you are going to need to be relevant. A lecture or hands-on exercise that is disconnected from your audience's lives is not going to be successful.

12.6
Phil Race's *The Lecturer's Toolkit: A Practical Guide to Learning, Teaching & Assessment*, 2nd ed. (London: Kogan Page, 2001) is a book I highly recommended (from the U.K.). The U.K.'s idea of a "lecturer" is not the American idea, so this is not a book about lecturing to your students, although it does discuss this teaching method. As it is both practical and forthright, you could recommend it to your teachers after you read it. It covers different learning styles and motivation for learning.

12.7
Involve your students and they are much more likely to understand what you are teaching them.

12.8
Some students are anxious about using the library. Your awareness of this should encourage you to be as welcoming and soothing as possible.

12.9
Some students are shy about approaching the reference desk staff. Let students know that staff want to help. If you have desk hours, mention that too.

12.10
Ask attendees to write things down. Depending on the topic, students will need to remember the titles of recommended indexes and databases, key terms that work in specific indexes, and call numbers and locations of useful books.

12.11
"People are able to recall:
"20% of what they read
"30% of what they hear
"40% of what they see
"50% of what they say
"60% of what they do
"90% of what they see, hear, say, and do."[1]

12.12
Repeat key points so that your students will be more likely to remember them. Write down the names of important indexes and databases.

12.13

"Be realistic about how much differentiation is manageable. In most situations, catering for three groups, higher, average, and lower attainers, is about as much as can be achieved."[2]

12.14

Do not try to reach all possible types of learners in one session. Offer to give individual assistance later.

12.15

See Linda B. Nilson, *Teaching at Its Best: A Research-Based Resource for College Instructors* (Bolton, Mass.: Anker, 1998), 63-8 for descriptions of Kolb and Fleming and Mills' learning styles, and multisensory teaching suggestions.

12.16

Try to "provide two or more areas in which to work with the participants—an essentially quiet one for those who cannot concentrate in the midst of discussion or activity, and an action-oriented area in which those who prefer active participation and sound can learn together."[3]

12.17

Because of time-of-day learning preferences, offer the same workshop at different times of the day.

12.18

Have students watch you conduct searches; have them do their own searches, let them help others with their searches. This will help them learn more thoroughly how to search library resources.

12.19

In the classroom, when you are teaching a group of unknowns—the usual librarian situation—remember to be unfailingly patient with students who speak slowly. Look attentive and alert. Do not sound or act impatient.

Myers-Briggs

12.20

The Myers-Briggs Type Indicator (MBTI) is a test that identifies a person's preferences—how he or she likes to work, relax, or learn. There are sixteen types and it is worth finding out what yours is. As a teacher you are not going to have information about each student, but knowing what preferences are out there can help direct your teaching style. Each person has a combination of letters that defines his or her type: INFJ, INFP, ENFJ, ENFP, INTJ, INTP, ENTJ, ENTP, ISTJ, ISFJ, ESTJ, ESFJ, ISTP, ISFP, ESTP, or ESFP. I is Introvert, E is extrovert, F is Feeling, N is iNtuition, S is Sensing, T is Thinking, J is Judging, and P is Perceiving. Someone with ST is a sensing thinker, NT is an intuitive thinker, etc.

12.21

Charles C. Schroeder: "In our initial studies, we focused most of our inquiry on two very broad learning patterns associated with sensing and intuition. The results indicate that approximately 60 percent of entering students prefer the sensing mode of perceiving compared to 40 percent who prefer the intuitive mode. The learning styles of those who prefer sensing are characterized by a preference for direct, concrete experiences; moderate to high degrees of structure; linear, sequential learning; and, often, a need to know why before doing something. In general, students who prefer sensing learning patterns prefer the concrete, the practical, and the immediate. These students often lack confidence in their intellectual abilities and are uncomfortable with abstract ideas. They have difficulty with complex concepts and low tolerance for ambiguity. Furthermore, they are often less independent in thought and judgement and more dependent on the ideas of those in authority. They are also more dependent on immediate gratification and exhibit more difficulty with basic academic skills, such as reading and writing. The path to educational excellence for sensing learners is usually a practice-to-theory route,—not the more traditional theory-to-practice approach. . . .

"Contrast the sensing learning patterns to those of the intuitives. They are generally global learners, 'big picture' types, who prefer to focus their perceptions on imaginative possibilities rather than on concrete realities. Intuitives love the world of concepts, ideas, and abstractions[.] Their path to excellence is from theory to practice, and they often prefer open-ended instruction to highly structured instruction. They usually demonstrate a high degree of autonomy in their learning and value knowledge for its own sake . . . intuitives prefer diversity in ideas and learning options [and] are not uncomfortable with ambiguity."[4]

12.22

"When comparing the preferred learning patterns of faculty to those of students, it is not surprising to find that faculty prefer the abstract reflective (IN) pattern. MBTI data collected over the years on faculty of numerous campuses reveal that over 75 percent of faculty prefer the intuitive learning pattern, with the vast majority of these preferring the abstract reflective (IN) pattern. On many of these campuses, fewer than 10 percent of faculty prefer the concrete active (ES) pattern."[5]

12.23
Keep in mind that your learning style may be different from your students.

12.24
Remain patient and courteous at all times. Be willing to talk more slowly and to repeat steps so students will not fall behind. Offer to help one on one outside of class time.

12.25
Have opportunities for students to work together. Have time when everyone is doing independent hands-on work. Give a well-organized presentation. Leave enough flexibility in your session to address the unexpected.

12.26
If your library session is late enough in the semester, ask the instructor what preferred methods of learning the students in the course have. The instructor may not have observed any, but if he or she has noticed, the information will be very useful for you.

12.27
Learning styles associated with the MBTI functions:
Different styles learn best by:
- ST: doing, hands-on activities
- SF: doing, hands-on activities with others
- NF: imagining, creating with others, writing
- NT: categorizing, analyzing, applying logic

Need:
- ST: precise, step-by-step instructions; logical, practical reasons for doing something
- SF: precise, step-by-step instructions; frequent friendly interaction and approval
- NF: general direction, with freedom to do it their own creative way; frequent positive feedback
- NT: to be given a big problem to solve, an intellectual challenge, and then to be allowed to work it out

They want from the teacher:
- ST: to be treated fairly
- SF: sympathy, support, individual recognition
- NF: warmth, enthusiasm, humor, individual recognition
- NT: to be treated with respect, to respect the teacher's competence[6]

12.28
See page 63 of Sandra Krebs Hirsh, *Using the Myers-Briggs Type Indicator in Organizations: Workshop Leaders' Guide,* 2nd ed. (Palo Alto, Calif.: Consulting Psychologists Press, 1991) for tips on teaching to types (pages 9-11). Page 64 has areas for skill development for each type.

North, South, East, and West

12.29
For additional useful advice for how to get along with others depending upon your own direction, see Diane Turner and Thelma Greco, *The Personality Compass: A New Way to Understand People* (Boston: Element, 1998). This book has an excellent summary of various learning styles and personality types as described by more than one researcher or set of researchers over centuries of years.

12.30
Personality types: North, East, South, and West
In brief:
North: natural leader, goal-centered, fast-paced, task-oriented, assertive, decisive, confident, determined, competitive, independent
East: natural planner, quality-centered, analytical, organized, logical, focused, exact, perfectionist, industrious, structured
South: natural team player, process-centered, slow-paced, good listener, non-confrontational, sensitive, patient, understanding, generous, helpful
West: natural risk-taker, idea-centered, creative, innovative, flexible, visionary, spontaneous, enthusiastic, free-spirited, energetic[7]

12.31
Norths as students (in general):
- "Know the answers frequently
- Express opinions openly
- Take a firm position on issues or ideas
- Prefer being 'right' to being 'popular'
- Challenge the instructor's knowledge
- Are usually in the middle of the action
- Find ways to get attention
- Get bored when work is slow and quiet
- Compete for top honors or recognition
- Do extra work just to stay busy
- Enjoy giving presentations in front of the class"

Easts as students (in general):
- "Ask detailed questions
- Are quick to point out errors made by instructors
- Become upset when discussions get off track
- Have little tolerance for exaggeration and inaccuracy . . .
- Take education seriously
- Argue over logical points and minutiae
- Come across as studious and intellectual
- Like to analyze reasons for everything
- Often confirm assignments with teachers after class
- Pay careful attention and stay focused"

Souths as students (in general):
- "Hesitate to speak out in class
- Trust others' opinions more than their own
- Avoid taking sides in controversial issues
- Aim to be liked, and are often popular
- Respect the instructor's authority
- Try not to be too noticeable
- Enjoy a slow-speed, relaxed environment
- Display very little competitive spirit
- Turn assignments in late at times
- Dread class presentations
- Say as little as possible in discussions
- Have many friends"

Wests as students (in general):
- "Look out the window and daydream a lot . . .
- Find any excuse to leave the classroom . . .
- Come up with the most and best ideas
- Like to 'doodle' as they try to listen
- Have trouble paying attention
- Take risks by talking and passing notes
- Enjoy being the class clown"[8]

Students with Disabilities

12.32
When communicating with deaf people:
- First get the person's attention.

- Look directly at him or her.
- Speak slowly and clearly.
- Maintain eye contact.
- Rephrase instead of repeating.

12.33
Offer to write down what you are saying. Then print clearly.

12.34
Being heard. If only one member of your audience cannot hear you, offer them a seat near the front. Do not ask them if they are deaf.

12.35
"It is the responsibility of a library patron or applicant or employee with a disability to make his or her disability known in order to enjoy equal access to the library facility, service, and programs."[9]

12.36
When teaching, mention any resources that you have to help students with disabilities. Do this in a general way, so no one student is singled out.

12.37
Mention ways to increase font size on screens.

12.38
If you work with deaf children, Marc Marschark, Harry G. Lang, and John A. Albertini, *Educating Deaf Students: From Research to Practice* (Oxford: Oxford University Press, 2002) is recommended. Page 72 has a thoughtful summary of how to communicate with young deaf children.

12.39
If you work in a library that serves visually impaired or blind students, Shonda Brisco, "From Braille to Zoom Text: Resources to Meet the Needs of Blind or Visually Impaired Students in the Media Center," *Library Media Connection,* August/September 2003: 50-3, lists a number companies (with Web sites when available) who sell useful resources.

12.40
When serving patrons with disabilities, offer to help, just as you would any other patron. Never presume that the person needs a specific type of assistance.

12.41
Courtney Deines-Jones and Connie Van Fleet, *Preparing Staff to Serve Patrons with Disabilities: A How-to-Do-It Manual*, How-to-Do-It Manuals for Librarians 57 (New York: Neal-Schuman, 1995) is a useful book worth reading if you have a significant population of disabled people (significant could mean one). Page 2 has a good outline of general advice.

Learning Differences

12.42
Characteristics of visual, auditory, and haptic (physical) learners.
"Visual Learners: Indications
"Visual learners need to see it to know it. They have a strong sense of colour and often have artistic ability. Visual learners have difficulty with spoken directions, and hence have trouble following lectures, and may misinterpret words and overreact to sounds in general.
"Suggestions: Well organized graphics help visual learners to learn and remember. Colour coding can assist with organizing notes and research material for essays and assignments. Written directions are essential. Visualization aids retention of facts and the correct spelling of words. Flow charts and diagrams assist notetaking.
"Auditory Learners: Indications
"Auditory learners are good listeners; they need to hear it to know it. Reading, writing, and following written directions are usually problematic. Auditory learners have trouble accurately assessing body language and correctly interpreting facial expressions.
"Suggestions: Taped texts, articles, lecture notes, and other class material are helpful. Auditory learners learn well through discussion and in participatory settings, e.g. seminars. Having material read aloud aids the revision/correction process in essays . . .
"Haptic (Physical) Learners: Indications
"Physical learners have to do it to know it. They have difficulty sitting still, and learn better when physical activity is involved. They may be well-coördinated and athletic.
"Suggestions: Experiential, interactive learning formats work best for these students. Reading, reciting, memorizing, and drilling while exercising aids retention and memory, e.g., reading while riding a stationary bike, listening to taped material while jogging. Using a computer to make study notes, revise lecture notes, etc. is a learning aid for physical learners."[10]

12.43
When designing facilities remember to consider health and safety requirements.

Non-Traditional Students

12.44
Returning students have concerns about all of the changes in libraries since they were last in school. Reassure them that there are people in the library who are happy to help them. Offer workshops aimed at these students so they can feel that they are in a comfortable learning environment with others in similar stages of life.

12.45
Encourage returning students to apply their life experiences to their research. If they have ever purchased a car, house, or major appliance, they have most likely been using forms of critical thinking—even if it was only comparing prices to the contents of their wallets and/or bank accounts.

12.46
Older students sometimes contribute valuable insights about the importance of good research to the class at large. This reinforces what you are doing.

12.47
Non-traditional students are some of the most enjoyable students to teach. They tend to be interested in your presentation, will ask questions (with the exception of the very shy), and will later follow up at the reference desk.

High-Risk/Gifted Students

12.48
"Seven learning style traits significantly discriminate between high-risk students or dropouts and students who perform well in school. A majority of dropouts and underachievers need:
- frequent opportunities for mobility;
- choices;
- a variety of instructional resources, environments, and sociological groupings, rather than routines and patterns;
- to learn during late morning, afternoon, or evening hours, but not in the early morning;
- informal seating; not wooden, steel, or plastic chairs;
- low illumination (bright light contributes to their hyperactivity); and
- tactual/visual introductory kinesthetic/visual resources reinforced by tactual/visual resources."[11]

12.49

When teaching, "gifted and underachieving students generally should not be grouped together because they learn through significantly different learning styles." (Conclusion derived from "study of adolescents in nine culturally diverse nations.")[12]

12.50

A lot of information on learning styles is distilled in the short package of Rita Dunn's *Strategies for Educating Diverse Learners*. I recommend reading it.

12.51

Keep in mind that "both non-academic and academic students achieve higher quality learning outcomes under active teaching methods than under passive methods, but that non-academic students stand to gain more in improved quality of learning from more active teaching methods than do academic students."[13]

12.52

Include pictures and other types of graphics to help explain concepts to students who learn best from images, not text. This may be difficult in a library setting because the majority of what we are searching and finding is text based.

K-12/Adult Differences

12.53

"Children need to feel physically comfortable if they are to concentrate on, process, internalize, and remember new and difficult information or skills. Individuals' comfort levels are determined by their reactions to their learning environment; sound versus quiet, bright lights versus soft illumination; warm versus cool; formal seating versus informal seating, mobility versus passivity, and intake (something to eat, chew, or drink) while learning."[14]

12.54

K-12 students learn best in a variety of ways:
- Alone (at least 13%)
- In pairs
- In teams working together
- In teams competing against one another
- With an adult

12.55
Remember that there are students who have learned a great deal via lectures over the years! They may be in a minority, but they are still around.

12.56
28% of elementary school students are early birds.
30% of junior high school students are early-morning workers. The "majority work best in late morning and early afternoon."
40% of high school students have early-morning preference—the rest prefer late morning and early afternoon.
"About 13% of high school students work best in the evening."
55% of adults are morning people.
28% of adults are best in the evening, with energy lows in the afternoon.
Worst mismatch is in high schools with it being unlikely that the teachers and students have high energy levels at the same time of day.[15]

12.57
"Get down to their level. When working with small children, they often seem to feel more comfortable when you're on their level, rather than physically, and possibly metaphorically, talking down to them. Making eye contact will often be easier when you're sitting in a low chair or kneeling beside them."[16]

Notes

1.   Eleri Sampson, *Creative Business Presentations: Inventive Ideas for Making an Instant Impact* (London: Kogan Page, 2003), 23.
2.   Nick Packard and Phil Race, eds., *2000 Tips for Teachers* (London: Kogan Page, 2000), 152.
3.   Rita Dunn, "Introduction to Learning Styles," in Rita Dunn and Kenneth Dunn, *The Complete Guide to the Learning Styles Inservice System* (Boston: Allyn and Bacon, 1999), 23.
4.   Charles C. Schroeder, "New Students – New Learning Styles," *Change* 25, no. 5 (1993): 21- . Read on http://www.virtualschool.edu/mon/Academia/KierseyLearningStyles.html (accessed May 26, 2004).
5.   Schroeder.
6.   Isabel Briggs Myers, rev. by Linda K. Kirby and Katharine D. Myers, *Introduction to Type: A Guide to Understanding Your Results on the* Myers-Briggs Type Indicator®, 6th ed. (Palo Alto, Calif.: Consulting Psychologists Press, 1998): 37.
7.   Diane Turner and Thelma Greco, *The Personality Compass: A New Way to Understand People* (Boston: Element, 1998), 19.
8.   Turner, 66, 118, 170, 222.
9.   Nancy C. Pack and Donald D. Foos, "Library Compliance with the Americans with Disabilities Act," *RQ* 32, no. 2 (1992): 260.

10. Patricia Brace, Rick Gordon, and Elizabeth Schumaker, *Writing & Students with Special Needs: A Manual for Writing Centre Tutors* (Kingston, Ontario: Queen's University, 1994), Appendix four.

11. Rita Dunn, *Strategies for Educating Diverse Learners.* FASTBACK® 384. (Bloomington, Ind.: Phi Delta Kappa Educational Foundation, 1995), 9.

12. Dunn, *Strategies*, 27.

13. Ross Guest, "The Instructor's Optimal Mix of Teaching Methods," *Education Economics* 9, no. 3 (2001): 315.

14. Dunn, *Strategies*, 11. Suggestions follow that apply mostly to K-6, but ideally could be applied to students in later years.

15. Dunn, *Strategies,* 17.

16. Packard & Race, 125.

13

Group Learning

Learning as part of a group can be effective, although it can be hard to imagine using up time in a brief one-time session on forming groups. However, there are instances when group activities will be the most instructive. This chapter talks about what to do if group activities are part of your teaching plans.

13.1
Some learners, particularly in early-morning classes, do not want to interact, so do not expect every group to respond positively to hands-on or small group exercises. Gauge the group beforehand by talking with the instructor first about student activities in the classroom. See also chapter 12 on ways students prefer to learn.

13.2
Do not create a group exercise just for the sake of doing it. Have an educational reason for it.

13.3
Collaborative learning: pairing students to coach one another. Work with the regular instructor to do this because this can be time consuming to set up.

13.4
When designing an exercise:
- How does it fit in with the rest of your session?
- Will you have enough time to cover all the needed material both before and after the exercise?

13.5
Choose the best size for the project at hand. A large group will not be able to see the same computer terminal or book. A small group may not be able to brainstorm as many ideas as a larger one.

13.6
Larger groups are probably not going to be an issue in library instruction sessions. Time to do tasks is limited and groups or two or three are probably going to be your best bet in most cases.

13.7
Create a checklist of intended outcomes before designing the exercise.

Forming Groups

13.8
Double discussion groups. Have students count off two numbers to ensure that the second group does not have any overlap with the first group. Or once the first group is assembled, have the students count off 1 to 4 or 1 to X to create the second group. (For example, count off 1 and 5, 2 and 6, 3 and 7, 4 and 8, 1 and 5, etc.)

13.9
"Students from cultures where the sexes do not often intermix . . . may be experiencing their first coeducational schooling. These students may thus be uncomfortable working together on a project with those of the opposite sex and may work better in single-sex groups."[1]

13.10
There are group size pluses and minuses. Read Phil Race, *500 Tips on Group Learning* (London: Kogan Page, 2000), pages142-4 for details on this.

13.11
Formation of groups. See details in Race, pages 144-8.
* Ways: friendship, geographical (as sitting/arranged in room), alphabetical (family name), other alphabetical (e.g., last letter of students' first names).
* Random: number—each student a number and tasks divided "1-4, 5-8 for task 1, then 1, 3, 5, 7; 2, 4, 6, 8 . . . then 1, 5, 9, 13 and so on" class-list rotating syndicates—printed list of class with "AAAA, BBBB, CCCC, DDDD . . . [then] ABCD, ABCD, ABCD . . . so everyone is in an entirely new group."

- Astrological—calendar month of birthdate, star signs (although group sizes will vary and transfers needed). "Participants from some religions may also find the method bizarre or inappropriate."
- Crossovers "ask one person from each group to move to another group." (earliest birthday in year . . . then latest in year).
- Coded name labels—names on labels with codes already on. "A three-digit code of a Greek letter, normal letter, and a number . . . possibility of . . . three completely different groups."
- Performance-related groups—ability ranges; skills-based groups—have "at least one member with identified skills and competencies."[2]

13.12
Form small groups—use a deck of cards (take out extras if fewer than 52—have more than one deck for larger groups). You can then have those with a certain number in a group, divide into four groups by suit, two groups red and black. Many other variations are possible.[3]

13.13
Use colored pieces of paper cut into different shapes—squares, circles, rectangles, triangles. Write numbers and/or letters on the paper and you have many additional possible configurations.

13.14
Give handouts with different colors, shapes, sizes, and materials (metal, plastic, plastic on metal) of paper clips and divide up groups based on type of clip. Or staple sheets together in different corners (or not in corners, on edge).

13.15
Mix up your handouts that have different specific tasks on them. After they have been handed out, groups are formed based on who got which task(s). Put a letter or number on the pages so that it is faster for participants to know to which group they belong.

13.16
In a one-time library session it is more important to form groups quickly than to use a creative, but slow method.

Pre-Activity

13.17
Plan your activity carefully. The timing and outcomes should make sense in the context of your session.

13.18
Make sure that there is a specific skill or task to be learned. Let students know what it is. For example, be able to locate the call number on catalog records; identify the probable bias in an article on a controversial topic.

13.19
It will take longer than you might expect for groups to complete an exercise. However, keep an eye out and if they finish sooner, move on to the reporting stage.

13.20
Be certain to create specific, accomplishable tasks. Write them out. For example:
- Create three difference searches using Boolean logic.
- List two ways that preferred terms are identified in indexes/databases.

13.21
Limit the number of expected outcomes to a manageable number. It is better that students gain a firm grasp of fewer concepts than a shaky grasp on many.

13.22
Have the task written down on the board or in a handout shared with the each group. Your verbal instructions may not be heard or understood clearly by everyone.

13.23
Describe the task in more than one way. Avoid jargon.

13.24
Intersperse the group activities with lectures and demonstrations. Be prepared to alter the next part of your session to respond to questions or concerns raised by the exercise.

13.25
Be careful not to set up a group exercise and then reveal the result before the groups have had a chance to work on it.

13.26

If individual groups need hints to get going, provide them in a timely enough fashion so that the group does not lag behind the others.

13.27

Have a classroom environment where mistakes are allowed. A test question or task that you do as an entire class can help put the students at their ease.

13.28

Before planning an exercise, make sure that there is enough room (physical space) for groups to work together. If groups are too close together they will have difficulty focusing.

13.29

If you have more than one classroom available you can send some groups to this other space. Be sure to visit every group at least once while they are doing their task, so no group feels isolated.

13.30

If you know in advance that you will be having a large number of groups and/or groups working in different locations, ask a colleague to join the session to help out.

13.31

Put the simple tasks first. Early success helps build group confidence.

13.32

Encourage everyone to participate! There is no point in assigning a group exercise if only one or two members work on it.

13.33

Let everyone know how the reporting stage will be done before they begin their task. That way they should be prepared for it—and it may help them complete their task.

13.34

Be sure to leave enough time for discussion or your audience will feel cheated. If you have designed a good exercise, people will want to talk about it with the entire class.

13.35

After the groups have had a chance to start their project, ask them for a brief report of where they are in the exercise to make sure they are on track.

13.36

Assign tasks within the group. For example, in a group of four, one student can read the question, a second can serve as keyboarder, a third as the recorder of the results, and the fourth can report the findings to the entire class.

13.37

"Help the shy or retiring students to have equal opportunity to contribute. Asking students in large groups to write questions, or ideas, on Post-its helps to ensure that the contributions you receive are not just from those students who are not afraid to ask in public."[4]

13.38

Use phases that encourage broader participation. Look at and smile at those who have not yet contributed and mention that their ideas are valuable too.

13.39

Encourage those who are not participating by giving general prompts. Ask if someone who has not spoken yet can provide another example (e.g., another way to arrange books—color, size, etc.).

13.40

After all of the groups have reported to the entire class, ask if anyone has anything to add.

13.41

Ask for someone to summarize what everyone has learned. You might assign this task before the groups give their reports.

13.42

Phil Race in *500 Tips for Group Learning* discusses bad group behaviors and ways to cope with them in chapters 32-36, pages 91-117.

Chapter 32 "Group member behaviours that damage group work" e.g. being late, not turning up at all, not prepared, etc. [91-8]

Chapter 33 "Group facilitator behaviours that can damage group work" e.g. ignoring non-participants, intimidating learners, lack of clear objectives, etc. [99-109]

Chapter 34 "Institutional factors that can damage group work" e.g. lack of suitable spaces, etc. [110-13]

Chapter 35 "Conflict in group work" [114-5]

Chapter 36 "Gender issues in group work" [116-7][5]

13.43

See pages 159-69 in Race, *The Lecturer's Toolkit* for group member problems and solutions.

Example Methods

13.44

"Think-pair-share is a simple cooperative learning exercise. The instructor asks a question or poses a problem. Students spend a minute or two *thinking* about an answer or solution. Students then *pair* up to discuss (*share*) their answers. The instructor then may ask for several students to *share* their answers with the whole class."[6]

13.45

"Jigsaw: Each member of the team is randomly assigned material to master and on which to become an 'expert.' Each expert briefs team members on that portion of the common topic."[7]

13.46

Jigsaw in action:

"Step 1: The instructor organizes the class into heterogeneous 'home' groups. A class might have 4-6 members per team depending on overall class size and numbers of tasks to be mastered. . . . Letters are given to each home group member so they can be easily identified.

"Step 2: Students reorganize to form 'expert' groups where they will work together to learn their subject material. For example, all the As join together. . . .

"Step 3: Students return to their home groups and take turns teaching their material to one another.

"Step 4: Students evaluate their group experience and discuss what could be done differently next time. The instructor may set an assignment or a quiz to allow each group an opportunity to apply what they have learned in a holistic manner."[8]

13.47

"A jigsaw procedure lessens the impact of disparities in ability among students by breaking the overall task into pieces and distributing a different piece to each small group of students."[9]

13.48

"Student demonstrations can be a quick way to make a point more vivid, give students a chance to hear from their peers, and give everyone in the class a 'think break.' The volunteer . . . [is] not the only one mulling over what he would do. . . . Each student in the room [is] asking himself or herself the same question. . . . So although only one or a handful of students may participate physically in the demonstration, the whole class has a chance to participate mentally."[10]

13.49
Pause procedure. Stop the lecture every thirteen to eighteen minutes to look over/rewrite notes and compare notes.[11]

13.50
"Focused listing, which could be used at any time during the course of a lecture, is designed to see whether students recall the most important points associated with a particular topic."[12]

13.51
An example of a library-related focused listing (indexes 1 and 3 are electronic):

	Advantages	Disadvantages	Comments
Index #1	Available remotely	Limited to only one user at a time	Includes images
Index #2 (print)	Can easily skim alphabetically nearby topics	Not available remotely	Use abbreviation interpretation pages
Index #3	Has full-text articles	Interface difficult to use	Multiple subjects covered

13.52
There are several good discussion-fostering ideas worth reading about in Timothy D. Green, "Responding and Sharing: Techniques for Energizing Classroom Discussions," *Clearing House,* July/August 2000: 331-4. It discusses seven techniques, with descriptions of how discussions are encouraged, teacher role, and challenges when using the specific technique:
Technique #1: Turn-to-Your-Neighbor
Technique #2: Think-Pair-Share
Technique #3: Think-Pair-Square-Share
Technique #4: Round Robin
Technique #5: Inside-Outside Circles
Technique #6: Line-Ups
Technique #7: Value Lines

Virtual Groups

13.53

Create a Frequently Asked Questions (FAQ) list that is accessible outside of the programming so that students will have access to it even when they are unable to log into their classroom account.

13.54

Include contact information for your institution's technical experts. In some cases, the problem will be outside of your scope to fix.

13.55

I recommend not requiring students to share photographs of themselves. Make it optional.

13.56

Develop (credited) easy projects that encourage interaction between students at the beginning of the course. Let them get accustomed to the software and communications mechanisms while the stakes are low.

13.57

"Set some simple tasks early on. . . .

"Give everyone some practice at using computer conferencing. . . .

"Put out some important information only by e-mail or in conferences to make people check for it. . . .

"Make sure some kind of backup is available. . . . Some sort of safety net could be used; for example, you could send out a message to all learners every week. Anybody who didn't receive the message would know to contact you so that you could try again or send a paper copy to them in the normal mail."[13]

13.58

While everyone shares responsibility for the results, if you assign a lengthy project, appoint one member as leader (rotate). A group leader is probably not needed for small projects.

Library Setting

13.59

Do group exercises only when you have the time. In a short session it can be much more efficient to demonstrate skills and call on one student at a time than to spend precious class time forming groups.

13.60

As the guest speaker, you will want to run your idea for a group exercise by the regular instructor during the early preparation stages.

13.61

As a guest lecturer it is not your role to produce class camaraderie. Your goal is to teach your students how to use the library to complete their assignment. If a group exercise supports that goal, by all means have one.

13.62

If you are not comfortable with creating or including group exercises (and want to integrate them into your teaching) ask colleagues for their ideas (library periodicals have examples too). Ask if you can observe a classroom where group learning is in action.

13.63

You might choose to have group learning as part of a team teaching effort. That way there is someone else to go around the room and give hints and help and everyone gets more attention.

Notes

1. Ellen Johnson, "Cultural Norms Affect Oral Communication in the Classroom," in *Approaches to Teaching Non-Native English Speakers across the Curriculum*, New Directions for Teaching and Learning, no. 70, eds. David L. Sigsbee, Bruce W. Speck, and Bruce Maylath (San Francisco: Jossey-Bass, 1997), 50. The entire chapter is useful.

2. Phil Race, *The Lecturer's Toolkit: A Practical Guide to Learning, Teaching & Assessment*, 2nd ed. (London: Kogan Page, 2001), 145-7.

3. John W. Newstrom and Edward Scannell, *The Big Book of Presentation Games: Wake-Em-Up Tricks, Ice Breakers, & Other Fun Stuff* (New York: McGraw-Hill, 1998), 117.

4. David Anderson, Sally Brown, and Phil Race, *500 Tips for Further and Continuing Education Lecturers* (London: Kogan Page, 1998), 33.

5. Phil Race, *500 Tips on Group Learning* (London: Kogan Page, 2000), 89.

6. Elisa Carbone, *Teaching Large Classes: Tools and Strategies,* Survival Skills for Scholars, vol. 19 (Thousand Oaks, Calif.: Sage Publications, 1998), 52.

7. David Royse, *Teaching Tips for College and University Instructors: A Practical Guide* (Boston: Allyn and Bacon, 2001), 83.

8. Corinne Laverty, "The Cooperative Jigsaw: A New Approach to Library Learning," in *New Ways of "Learning the Library"—and Beyond: Papers and Sessions Material Presented at the Twenty-third National LOEX Library Instruction Conference*

Held in Denton, Texas, 5 to 6 May 1995, ed. Linda Shirato, Elizabeth R. Bucciarelli, and Heidi Mercado (Ann Arbor, Mich.: Pierian Press, 1996), 116.

9.   David V. Perkins and Renee N. Saris, "A 'Jigsaw Classroom' Technique for Undergraduate Statistics Courses," *Teaching of Psychology,* May 2001: 111.

10.   Carbone, 54-5.

11.   Tracey E. Sutherland and Charles C. Bonwell, eds., *Using Active Learning in College Classes: A Range of Options for Faculty,* New Directions for Teaching and Learning, no. 67 (San Francisco: Jossey-Bass, 1996). Various chapters.

12.   Charles C. Bonwell, "Enhancing the Lecture: Revitalizing a Traditional Format," in *Using Active Learning in College Classes: A Range of Options for Faculty,* New Directions for Teaching and Learning, no. 67, eds. Tracey E. Sutherland and Charles C. Bonwell (San Francisco: Jossey-Bass, 1996), 36.

13.   Race, *Group Learning,* 83.

14

Evaluation Feedback Improving

Great teaching generally does not simply happen. It is learned; it is practiced. This chapter lists observable teaching behaviors and ways to gather opinions on what might need improvement.

14.1
If you get a chance to be taped teaching, take it! You do not need to show the video to anyone else (you should be able to notice the major glitches), but if you can, ask an experienced educator to help you with your teaching techniques.

14.2
Evaluations. Always use an odd-numbered scale: 3, 5, 7, etc., because people like a middle option.

14.3
Have a colleague sit in a class session and give you feedback.

14.4
Sit in on colleagues' sessions to get ideas for your own sessions.

14.5
Things an observer might notice:
- "Careful planning.
- Start (on time? brisk?).
- Pace (fast enough to maintain interest, but not lose students).
- Variety, length, and sequencing of activities.

- Creativity.
- Humor.
- Contextualizing of learning (how does this class fit into the larger context?).
- Participation (how many students? how substantial their output?).
- Style of dealing with questions.
- Style of dealing with challenges to authority.
- Ending (on time? 'not with a whimper but a bang'?)."[1]

14.6
Collecting evaluations can be a helpful way to garner input on your teaching.

14.7
"Assessment takes time, effort, and planning. It requires buy-in and support of one's own department and department head, colleagues in other departments, and administration. However, it does not need to be fancy. If one is fortunate enough to have campus support for statistical analysis one can do amazing things, but one can do equally valuable assessments with pencil and paper."[2]

14.8
The top seven good teaching traits have been identified as:
- "Student-Centered/Receptive
- Knowledgeable
- Effective Presenter
- Flexible/Creative
- Organized
- Enthusiastic
- Motivational"[3]

14.9
Judith M. Arnold's article, "I Know It When I See It: Assessing Good Teaching," *Research Strategies* 16, no. 1 (1998): 1-28, lists associated behaviors of the top seven good teaching traits in its appendix B (pages 17-25). These observable behaviors, such as "Responds to student questions/comments," could serve as a useful guide for a colleague observing library instruction sessions.

14.10
A peer observer can provide useful feedback about your teaching. One way to make this manageable and less threatening is for the teacher librarian to ask for feedback on only two or three specific teaching issues. For example, did the librarian move too quickly from screen to screen in the demonstration of the online catalog? Did students look like they were keeping up? An observer may

be able to see how the students appear to be reacting more easily than the person teaching.

14.11

An observer need not attend an entire session. For example, if beginnings or endings are the area of concern, the observer need only attend that portion of the session.

14.12

Take suggestions from public speaking courses for your own improvement. Have a colleague watch your delivery for:

- "Eye contact
- Vocal variety
- Adequate projection
- Appropriate rate
- Effective pauses
- Purposeful gestures
- Appropriate mannerisms
- Extemporaneous style"[4]

14.13

Visuals should be evaluated also. They need to be relevant, easy-to-see, clear, uncluttered, and used appropriately.

14.14

Ask about your responsiveness to questions. Did you appear to listen carefully? Answer the asked questions clearly? Look receptive to additional queries?

14.15

A good observer will praise strengths as well as provide suggestions for improvement. The help should be practical. If someone does not appear open for questions, an improvement would be recommending that after asking for questions the person pause and make eye contact with members of the class for at least ten full seconds before moving to the next point.

14.16

Include open-ended questions as well as yes/no and scale ratings.

14.17

An evaluation form should request input, thank the person filling it out, and tell him or her where to turn it in. Depending upon what is covered, you will want to vary the form. If you do not use a particular resource, there is no need to ask about it—unless you want to find out if you should have included it. This supposes your students already know something about it, which could be counterproductive.

14.18
Ask one question per question. Do not ask: "Was the instructor well prepared, organized, helpful, friendly, knowledgeable, ready, and comfortable with the technology?" Ask each element separately.

14.19
An area for open comments is highly recommended. Some of the most helpful (as in constructive and I could easily change or add it) feedback I have received over the years has been in this area. (For example, idea 4.34 of this book.)

14.20
You might move questions around and change what each side of the scales you use mean, to be sure that the responses are not automatic.

14.21
Below are some example evaluation questions that you can use or adapt (make blank lines longer in your versions, and leave enough space to write comments; people write with larger letters than you might expect). I suggest evaluation sheets for students have no more than seven questions and always ask for "comments/suggestions." Ideally the form should fit on half a sheet of paper. You could also create online evaluation forms, if you prefer.

Date:_____ Topic/Course: _____Librarian:_____
Please help us by taking a few moments to complete this evaluation form. All comments are welcome.
What did you find useful from this presentation?
Did you learn new ideas or skills? no yes
      If yes→ circle one: few some many
Please rate the extent to which you think this presentation will assist you in completing your assignment(s).
      Circle one: not at all=1 2 3 4 5=a lot
Amount of information was (Circle one):
      too little just right   too much
The librarian was knowledgeable about the subject matter:
      yes   somewhat   no
Was there adequate time for hands-on practice?
      Circle one: no by __ minutes   almost enough   enough
      too much by __ minutes

Librarian: well prepared   no   somewhat   yes
              knowledgeable about the subject   no   somewhat   yes
              encouraged and responded to questions   no   somewhat   yes
The material covered was:
    Circle one: too elementary   just right   too complex
Kind of information was:
    Circle one: too elementary   just right   too complex
Level of instruction was:
    Circle one: too elementary   just right   too complex
Handouts are clear:
    Circle one: not at all 1 2 3 4 5 to a large extent
Handouts are useful:
    Circle one: not at all 1 2 3 4 5 to a large extent
Visual aids (computer projections, transparencies, etc.) were clear:
    Circle one: not at all 1 2 3 4 5 to a large extent
Visual aids (computer projections, transparencies, etc.) enhanced the
presentation:
    Circle one: not at all 1 2 3 4 5 to a large extent
What I learned was worth the time invested:
    Circle one: not at all 1 2 3 4 5 to a large extent
Comments (for example, suggestions for improvement):
Thank you for your input! Please return this form to the librarian.

14.22
You might want to ask the instructor for specific types of input. For example:
1.   What did you find useful from the presentation?
2.   Did your students appear to learn new skills?
3.   Please rate the extent to which you think this presentation will assist
     students in completing their assignment(s):
         Circle one: not at all 1 2 3 4 5 to a large extent
4.   Amount of information was:
         too little just right   too much
5.   Level of instruction was:
         Circle one: too elementary   just right   too complex
6.   Librarian: well prepared no somewhat yes
              knowledgeable about the subject   no   somewhat   yes
              encouraged and responded to questions   no   somewhat   yes
7.   Visual aids (computer projections, transparencies, etc.) were clear:
         Circle one: not at all 1 2 3 4 5 to a large extent
8.   Visual aids (computer projections, transparencies, etc.) enhanced the
     presentation:
         Circle one: not at all 1 2 3 4 5 to a large extent
9.   Comments/suggestions

14.23

Even if you do not have an instructor provide formal feedback, before you teach the same session again ask for input on what worked and did not work. Does the instructor have any suggestions about what you should include? More hands on? Less? Should you cover more or fewer indexes?

14.24

There is no need to get feedback for every session. Evaluation uses valuable class time, and selective use is all that is needed. The teacher with little experience will need the most feedback, but occasional feedback remains helpful for the very experienced one.

14.25

After integrating a new technique, get comments on how it works before including it in future sessions.

14.26

Some libraries implement a formal process for evaluating teaching, but informal, non-threatening critiques are very helpful and are recommended whether or not a formal structure exists.

14.27

See Daniel R. Beerens, *Evaluating Teachers for Professional Growth: Creating a Culture of Motivation and Learning* (Thousand Oaks, Calif.: Corwin Press, 2000), pages 62-75 for suggestions of things to evaluate: planning and preparation, classroom environment (interaction with students), and instruction. Components of each are provided and descriptions of the element (such as teacher interaction with students) with levels of performance described (unsatisfactory, basic, proficient, distinguished). For example, proficient: "Teacher-student interactions are friendly and demonstrate general warmth, caring and respect."[5] Adapt elements to the library classroom—you are not going to be able to greatly impact student to student interactions in one session, so do not include that criterion in your librarian-teacher assessment (for guest teaching).

14.28

Talking with your colleague (librarian or other instructor) in advance of an evaluation or advisory observation is a useful way to set up peer evaluation. Discuss what you are trying to accomplish with the reviewer. Reviewer questions for the teacher might include:
1)   "What are the goals for the class I will observe?
2)   What are your plans for achieving these goals?
3)   What teaching/learning will take place?

4) What have students been asked to do in preparation for this class?
5) Will this class be typical of your teaching style? If not, why?
6) (For formative review) What would you like me to focus on during the observation?
7) Are there other things that I should be aware of prior to the observation?"[6]

14.29
See pages 91-4 of Nancy Van Note Chism, *Peer Review of Teaching: A Sourcebook* (Bolton, Mass.: Anker, 1999), for possible items for a peer evaluator to observe and rate on a scale in the classroom See page 90 for creating the scaled rating form. Be specific.

14.30
If you plan to have an in-depth teaching evaluation program, these two books (with chapters by different authors) are recommended:

- Katherine E. Ryan, ed., *Evaluating Teaching in Higher Education: A Vision for the Future,* New Directions for Teaching and Learning, no. 83 (San Francisco: Jossey-Bass, 2000)
- Christopher Knapper and Patricia Cranton, eds., *Fresh Approaches to the Evaluation of Teaching,* New Directions for Teaching and Learning, no. 88 (San Francisco: Jossey-Bass, 2001)

Notes

1. A. Clay Schoenfeld and Robert Magnan, *Mentor in a Manual: Climbing the Academic Ladder to Tenure,* 2nd ed. (Madison, Wis.: Atwood, 1994), 226.
2. Elizabeth W. Carter, "'Doing the Best You Can with What You Have:' Lessons Learned from Outcomes Assessment," *Journal of Academic Librarianship* 28, no. 1 (2002): 40.
3. Judith M. Arnold, "I Know It When I See It: Assessing Good Teaching," *Research Strategies* 16, no. 1 (1998): 8.
4. Karrin Anderson, *Speech Coursebook* (N.p.: Thomson Custom Publishing, 2003), 13.
5. Daniel R. Beerens, *Evaluating Teachers for Professional Growth: Creating a Culture of Motivation and Learning* (Thousand Oaks, Calif.: Corwin Press, 2000), 67.
6. Nancy Van Note Chism, *Peer Review of Teaching: A Sourcebook* (Bolton, Mass.: Anker, 1999), 81.

15

Promoting Library Instruction

While we might think that what we have to offer is terrific, sometimes a librarian needs to sell his or her product or service. Others, whose plates are quite full already (teaching many classes right now, thank you very much), are probably *not* going to want to generate additional interest. Here are ideas to start or increase the number of library instruction sessions you teach.

15.1
"School and academic libraries have a clearly specified role to play; they exist to support the missions of their parent institutions. Not only must these libraries define their role in support of the learning, teaching, and research functions of their institutions, but they also must make their faculties and administrators understand that role."[1]

15.2
Ideas to get a library instruction program started:
1. "Meet New Faculty . . .
2. Explain Library Service at Departmental Meetings . . .
3. Offer Faculty-Only Workshops in the Use of Research Resources . . .
4. Take Advantage of Faculty Retreats . . .
5. Join the Faculty Brown-Bag-Lunch Series . . .
6. Be Active in the 'Center for Teaching Excellence' . . .
7. Develop a Research Component for 'Writing Across the Curriculum' Workshops . . .
8. Write Articles in Professional Journals Other than Library Journals . . .
9. Attend Cultural and Social Events with Faculty . . .
10. Offer a Summer Institute."[2]

15.3
Promote your library instruction by different means:
- Brochures
- On your Web site
- At the reference desk
- Directly to instructors who give difficult library research assignments. Ask for instructors' names from the students

15.4
Brochures and flyers should look professional.

15.5
Only personalize brochures with librarian names and contact information if you can update them whenever there is a staff change. Web site contact information must also be kept current. If a potential client cannot find the librarian needed quickly, he or she may decide not to make the effort to request a session.

15.6
When contacted, respond as quickly as possible. A delay on your part may be interpreted as a lack of interest. Sometimes the call comes when the instructor is working on his or her syllabus and your lack of response may keep you off of it.

15.7
Align your library goals with the larger institutional unit (grade, junior/middle, or high school; university, city, district, corporation, etc.) and mention these goals when promoting your services.[3]

15.8
Instruction does not take place only in the classroom. Broaden your vision to include Web pages, handouts, tutorials, and whatever other means you can think of that will accomplish the needed goal.

15.9
Keep track of the classes you teach. Numbers can be an effective promotional tool. Statistics can be kept electronically. Include date, time, place, group/course name, instructor's name, and number of attendees. At the university level you might want to differentiate attendees between undergraduate and graduate students. At a public library you might want to differentiate between young children, teens, and adults.

15.10
Starting a library instruction program? Look at May Brottman and Mary Loe, eds., *The LIRT Library Instruction Handbook* (Englewood, Colo.: Libraries

Unlimited, 1990). It is a bit dated now, but it has some very useful information about starting a program in academic, public, school, and special libraries. There is an excellent bibliography.

University/College

15.11
Library research is not just for English and composition courses. Point out the benefits to faculty in all subject areas. History students need primary sources, psychology students need case studies, interior design students need examples, chemistry students need to find information about specific chemicals, etc.

15.12
Library instruction does not always need to be course related. Is there a new electronic index or content database that you want to promote? Offer a couple of sessions on searching it.

15.13
Offer sessions at night and on weekends. Sometimes that is the only available free time people have. Before committing yourself to a time, find out if there is any interest. It never hurts to ask!

15.14
Groups to be served by library instruction on a university campus include:
- Undergraduate students
- Graduate students
- Teaching assistants
- Research assistants
- Faculty
- Staff
- Library staff
- Community members
- Adjunct instructors
- Department chairs

Students might also be reached by other campus connections: athletics, interest groups (academic and social clubs or organizations either directly or indirectly sponsored by the parent organization), and degree programs are some of the ways you can try to reach students.

15.15
Ask your liaison or the departmental chair to invite you to departmental meetings. At the meeting, you can promote your instructional services.

15.16
Keep subject specialists' business cards at the reference desk to hand out to faculty and teaching assistants.

15.17
Send an e-mail before the beginning of a new semester to remind faculty about planning for library instruction.

15.18
Offer to teach library-related topics on a campuswide basis—at the university's computer lab.

15.19
If you are a department liaison, mention that you can provide library instruction when you meet with faculty about other topics (book or journal selection, indexes, databases, budget cuts, specialized reference assistance, etc.).

15.20
Put up flyers (clear these with the department first) in departmental mailbox and photocopy machine areas.

K-12

15.21
Be there on open school night or when parents are meeting teachers. Show off the library or media center while parents wait their turn or after their meeting. Roam the halls and tell parents about the media center and encourage them to visit. Make sure that you have someone friendly in the media center to greet those who stop by.

15.22
Offer to have teacher, parent-teacher, district, and board meetings in your library. Show off your facility and talk about your services before and after the meetings. Serve as a resource during the meetings. Have school statistics at your fingertips.

15.23
Create a library newsletter. Keep it brief enough to read in a few minutes.

15.24
Sponsor an open house for your faculty to show off your facility.

15.25
Go to people's work area or classroom to do your instruction.

15.26
Ask satisfied clients to speak on your behalf. "Board members and administrators expect the library media specialist to advocate for the library program, but when classroom teachers speak in your favor, it carries an extra endorsement."[4]

15.27
Become familiar with your local public and/or university libraries. Offer sessions to your students, their parents, and your teachers on what they can expect when they visit these libraries. Make sure you verify any facts that you might share with a librarian or two from the library you are describing.

15.28
Not all high school graduates (or dropouts) go to college. But they will need research skills to get them through life. Offer to teach life research: choosing automobiles, appliances, finding jobs, etc. Your audience is not solely the college-bound students.

Marketing/Promoting

15.29
Market to each group. Use individualized promotion for each.

15.30
Tell people that slots are filling quickly; this is a way to motivate them to make arrangements.

15.31
E-mail messages are another useful form of communication.

15.32
Use traditional corkboards to post flyers and updates of your library's instructional services.

15.33

When helping a faculty member or teaching assistant at the reference desk, promote your library instruction program.

15.34

Get your library's contact information into offices. One idea: a "business card-sized magnet with the research library's contact information on it." Include "phone and fax numbers, email address, and Web sites."[5]

15.35

Promote library instruction on your Web site. Have an electronic form to make requests for sessions.

15.36

Meet with faculty in their offices. Some teaching faculty will never visit the library. Bring the librarian to them. This also gives you opportunities to show off any remote access that you might have to your library.

15.37

When you meet with faculty in your office, show off your library classroom when you walk them out.

15.38

Introduce yourself to new faculty, teachers, etc. If the person you are talking with has a different departmental liaison, give them your colleague's name. Inform your colleague of the encounter so he or she may follow up. Promote library instruction to faculty you meet at lectures, open houses, in the student center, etc.

15.39

"Remember, it's not just about books or learning resources. It is even more important to establish your own credibility with academics, as someone who can support their teaching and who can help their students to learn effectively and efficiently."[6]

15.40

Librarians are selling high-quality student projects. Achieve that product via:
- Library instruction session
- Web page customized for the assignment
- Handout with bibliography (can include URLs)
- One-to-one assistance at reference desk or in office

15.41

Sell your valuable service at every opportunity. Good libraries have a wide variety of materials, so you should have something for everyone.

15.42

You never are "off." If you meet a potential client in the grocery store, make your pitch there and/or offer to meet with them in your office later. Keep it brief, but all meetings have potential.

15.43

If you act bored or speak in a flat monotone when speaking with instructors, no one is going to want you to speak for ten minutes in front of their students, never mind for an entire class session. Sound and act lively when promoting your services.

15.44

Share a common interest in the importance of solid research with your teaching faculty. Find out where the gaps in students' projects are, and talk about how they can be addressed through your instruction. The time spent on it is well worth it in the long haul—even a brief class session will introduce the students to their librarian. Ask to set a date for the session. Prepare and deliver a well-organized and useful presentation.

15.45

Listen very carefully to what faculty members say about their research. You may discover ways you can be helpful that go beyond offering to teach a class. This other assistance gives you additional opportunities to promote other library services, including, of course, library instruction.

15.46

Make sure your promotional materials have a specific audience in mind.

15.47

Address your audience's research needs. Then talk about how your library can help.

15.48

Proofread everything! You will not be credible if your materials are filled with spelling or other errors.

15.49

When you publish "stories in campus newspapers (both official and student) and library and computer center newsletters [they] are helpful but they need to be done *regularly* because of the changes in the student, faculty, and staff populations."[7]

15.50

See if you can get a regular column in a departmental newsletter. This way you can promote the new (or inform of the removed) library materials. Use the column to teach people how to use databases (covert library instruction). In the signature line include all of the services you provide, including instruction.

15.51

Be ready to teach about the library on short notice. Keep a generic outline that can be quickly adapted. But do not encourage short notice! Make certain that you say that this is a special exception and to plan ahead next semester. You must be sure that others agree that your time is as valuable as theirs or you risk losing stature at your institution, not to mention your sanity.

Promote Value

15.52

Remind instructors and faculty of the value of a guest librarian. "Occasionally scheduling a guest lecturer can be a good pedagogical technique for three reasons. First, students like variety; they like to hear other perspectives. Second, guest lecturers are usually chosen because they are especially knowledgeable about a particular topic and can supplement textbooks or readings where coverage is less than adequate. Third, guest lecturers are role models—generally they are individuals who have become successful and are recognized for their accomplishments."[8] As a librarian, you are the local library research expert.

15.53

"Students who master information literacy skills in secondary school perform significantly better in higher education. They also become informed consumers, community advocates, and contributing members of the workforce as adults."[9]

15.54

"Well-chosen guest lecturers can validate the importance of knowing the very items you have been struggling to get across."[10] It is also very hard for instructors to keep up-to-date with everything that is going on in the library. Therefore, inviting a librarian to cover library-related topics can be welcome.

15.55

"In 'real life,' as the commencement orators so often refer to the years after graduation, there is no reserve shelf."[11]

15.56

First, "a good learning experience imitates reality. Once students graduate, no one is going to stop work to lecture them each time they need to learn something new for their jobs. No one is going to hand them a textbook or reading list. No one is going to put books on reserve for them in the public library. Traditional teaching methods no longer apply.

"If, however, while in school, people have gained an awareness of the information resources in their fields, learned how to access them, to evaluate them, and to use them effectively, they will be well prepared for the post-graduation, real-life situations they encounter. Library-based instruction can prepare people to cope with the multimedia and computer information that is so much a part of society today. It can prepare them to screen and employ effectively the mass media that bombards them everywhere they go. Faculty and librarians working together can help students learn how to deal with the realities of the world's vast, multitudinous store of information."[12]

15.57

Research skills apply across a wide range of libraries and research needs. The skills gained in an instructional session will often apply to future assignments.

15.58

Attending more than one library instruction session can reinforce concepts learned in previous ones. Some students need to have something described more than one way and/or need more practice using a skill. One library session per degree program will probably not answer all research questions.

Notes

1. Patricia Senn Breivik, *Planning the Library Instruction Program* (Chicago: American Library Association, 1982), 1.

2. Rosemary M. Young and Stephena Harmony, *Working with Faculty to Design Undergraduate Information Literacy Programs: A How-to-Do-It Manual for Librarians*, How-to-Do-It Manuals for Librarians 90 (New York: Neal-Schuman, 1999), 22-4.

3. Steven M. Baule and Laura Blair Bertani, "How to Gain Support from Your Board and Administrators: Marketing 101 for Your Library Media Program," *Book Report*, November/December 2000: 47.

4. Baule, 49.

5.   Kristine D. Dworkin, "Library Marketing: Eight Ways to Get Unconventionally Creative," *Online,* January/February 2001: 54. Especially useful article for corporate librarians trying to promote all of their services (not just instruction).

6.   Sally Brown, Bill Downey, and Phil Race, *500 Tips for Academic Librarians* (London: Library Association Publishing, 1997), 100-1.

7.   Douglas Ferguson, "Marketing Online Services in the University," *Online,* 1 no. 3 (1977): 19.

8.   David Royse, *Teaching Tips for College and University Instructors: A Practical Guide* (Boston: Allyn and Bacon, 2001), 74.

9.   Alicia Cornelio, "Promoting Information Literacy through Information Architecture," *Library Media Connection,* March 2003, 24.

10.   Royse, 74.

11.   Henry M. Wriston, *Academic Procession: Reflections of a College President* (New York: Columbia University Press, 1959), 137.

12.   Gordon E. Gee and Patricia Senn Breivik, "Libraries and Learning," in *Libraries and the Search for Academic Excellence. Proceedings of the Arden House Symposium* (New York, NY; March 15-17, 1987) [See IR 052 055. ERIC ED 284 593], 14.

16

Distance Education

Teaching the library from a distance presents its own challenges. Whether you are giving a guest lecture for a distance course (via television, WebCT, Blackboard, or equivalent) or the principal instructor yourself, there are time-consuming considerations that you need to address before you teach. This chapter gives general advice on teaching at a distance.

16.1
"Prospective students need to know that a distance course requires self-discipline, self-motivation, the ability to work independently, and perseverance."[1]

16.2
Present things visually as much as possible. Show what the buttons from recommended indexes look like. Display screen shots of the online catalog and databases. Show the sequence from library home page to the opening page of a resource.

16.3
Read Thomas C. Cyrs, ed., *Teaching and Learning at a Distance: What It Takes to Effectively Design, Deliver and Evaluate Programs,* New Directions for Teaching and Learning, no. 71 (San Francisco: Jossey-Bass, 1997) if you will be teaching a credit course on television.

On Television: In General

16.4

Television and computer screens will tend to be smaller than what you can project in a classroom, so a large, clean font style and only a few words per screen is desirable.

16.5

Type your notes in a large font on numbered pages (in case they drop). Leave the bottom quarter or third of the page blank, so you are not looking down in a conspicuous manner.

16.6

In my "Teaching the Library and Electronic Resources on Television," in *"LOEX" of the West: Teaching and Learning in a Climate of Constant Change*, Foundations in Library and Information Science, vol. 34, ed. Thomas W. Leonhardt (Greenwich, CT: JAI Press, 1996), I describe a number of things that I found helpful when I was teaching a credit course on television. Some of the ideas in this chapter are taken or adapted from this resource, but there are additional specific ideas in it.

16.7

Be your own director when you can. Give cues to the camera operator(s).

16.8

Include photographs of the outside and sections within your library. Have a floor plan available so you can show where the photograph was taken.

16.9

Say step-by-step details. "Now I am pressing return," just as you would in an all-live classroom.

16.10

Make sure that your presentation slides have a large enough type size to display well on television: 48 to 72 points is recommended.

16.11

Use single, light-colored backgrounds because colors get distorted and can shimmer over the air.

16.12

You will need to adapt all of your preexisting handouts before you can use them on television. At minimum, type sizes will need to be increased.

16.13

Before you teach:

"Spend a few minutes prior to your presentation with the equipment operator or technician to discuss what assistance you may need during your lecture. . . . A technician should be notified prior to the presentation of your intent to use audiovisual materials to assure that the format of the information is of broadcast quality when received at the distant sites."[2] Experiment days, not hours, in advance of when you plan to use audiovisual material.

16.14

Speak in your normal classroom voice when on television. Your microphone projects your voice onto the air. You will appear foolish if you speak too loudly.

16.15

"On television, it is critical that the presenter keeps eye contact with the camera and that he or she smiles, articulates well, and uses voice modulation."[3]

16.16

If not predetermined, find out what the TV width of the chalkboard is, so you will stay within proper frame boundaries.

16.17

If at all possible, arrange for a trial run. Do a session seen only by you and the camera operator to get accustomed to the layout of the room, the number of cameras, and where they are found, what you look like, what your visuals look like, etc. If you have the nerve, have someone else watch the tape and give you suggestions.

16.18

Talk with your institution about copyright and over the air issues. See Joanis H. Bruwelheide, "Copyright: Opportunities and Restrictions for the Teleinstructor," in Thomas C. Cyrs, ed. *Teaching and Learning at a Distance: What It Takes to Effectively Design, Deliver and Evaluate Programs,* New Directions for Teaching and Learning, no. 71 (San Francisco: Jossey-Bass, 1997), 95-101. This chapter has an outline of several issues. Laws and practices may have changed since the chapter was written, but the issues have not.

16.19

The lighting for education TV can be wildly unflattering, so most people will want to wear at least minimal makeup. However, do not overdo it. If you can have more than one trial run with different makeup, take advantage of it so you can experiment with colors and amounts. You do not want your medium (you looking pale or ill or overdone) to interfere with your message. Just as in person, you do not want your makeup to be noticed when teaching or giving a talk.

16.20
Do not wear shiny or distracting jewelry.

16.21
Wear pastel colors with different textures.

16.22
Small patterns can look busy or make your viewers dizzy, so stick with monochrome tops. This applies to ties also—plain is better!

16.23
If you wear glasses, prefer smaller lenses to larger ones.

16.24
If you tend to be nervous and lean back, invest in the special coating on glasses that reduces glare from overhead lights. You want your viewers to see your eyes, not rectangular lights over your eyes. When you become relaxed enough to lean forward you can skip the special coating when you get a new prescription.

16.25
More clothing recommendations:
- "Do not wear white. Like scanning a graphic image on white paper, the clothing will create 'hot spots' or picture flare due to the stark contrasts creating light or dark areas on the screen. . . .
- Try to avoid wearing photosensitive glasses as they will darken under bright camera lights.
- Wear clothes with clean lines and classical styling that won't be dated.
- Choose light pastel colors with solid medium blue or grey suits. Pale shirts with colored ties in a conservative pattern are recommended."[4]

As Course Instructor on Television

16.26
If you only have two or three remote sites, have students call in before class for roll call, any questions, etc. This will help give the students confidence in calling in. During class time address them specifically.

16.27
Create a clear and detailed syllabus. Distance students will not have before- or after-class opportunities for informal interaction with you. Nor do you want to spend excessive amount of time via e-mail clarifying things.

16.28
Include detailed information about course requirements, due dates, and expectations for feedback and other types of participation on the syllabus. Be clear about any differences regarding assignments or participation for classroom and distance students.

16.29
Be willing to flex your assignments for distance students with limited (because small or afar) or no access to a physical library. Subject encyclopedias may need to be examined at a distance, for instance.

16.30
Include the slides (handout sized) in the students' textbook so they do not need to copy the screens.

16.31
Plan everything in advance! Handouts need to be mailed in advance or included in the textbook.

16.32
Have distance students answer questions on debatable topics before class time so their input can be included.

16.33
Talk directly to the distance students. Do not only make references and remarks to your in-class audience. Address distance students by name or nickname. Ask in your initial query how they would like to be addressed. They might be older or younger than you are or from a different culture with a different degree of formality or informality. Respect these differences.

16.34
Encourage your distance students to correspond via e-mail so their input can be included in as timely a fashion as possible.

16.35
Do not forget to address the students in the room!

16.36
Note: some of your in-class students will watch the monitor instead of looking at you live.

16.37
If you can visit a remote site, do so to meet your students in person.

16.38
Blue and green clothing can look alike on TV, so do not wear blue and green outfits on corresponding days.

16.39
If videotapes are made of the session, send in-class students who have missed class to watch them—there is no need for you to repeat your lecture. Then questions will be for clarification, not starting at the beginning.

Computer Instruction

16.40
There are limiting factors in WebCT/Blackboard-type systems. Slow modems mean best pedagogical practices may need to be abandoned when giving audio/presentation software lectures. Presentation slides between topics may not be an option because each slide needs to stay on the screen for a certain amount of time.

16.41
Do not write out a script; work from an outline. However, do practice saying things aloud before you get recorded.

16.42
Stay with plain and standard font styles on your presentation slides. In some cases the viewable screen will be smaller than monitor size.

16.43
Make screen snapshots of catalogs and databases and include them in your presentation slides. Use arrows to point out specific parts of the image, so you can refer to them while you are being recorded.

16.44
Break your talks into mini-lectures so students can repeat sections that are unclear to them without having to repeat parts they understood the first time.

16.45
Include contact information, especially an e-mail address, in your presentation, even when you are a guest speaker for a course. Students will then be able to contact you directly with their research questions (they do ask for advice).

Notes

1.   Darcy Walsh Hardy and Mary H. Boaz, "Learner Development: Beyond the Technology," in *Teaching and Learning at a Distance: What It Takes to Effectively Design, Deliver and Evaluate Programs,* New Directions for Teaching and Learning, no. 71, ed. Thomas C. Cyrs (San Francisco: Jossey-Bass, 1997), 45.

2.   Ann Pederson, "Teaching Over an Interactive Video Network," in *The Impact of Technology on Library Instruction: Papers and Session Materials Presented at the Twenty-first National LOEX Library Instruction Conference Held in Racine, Wisconsin, 14 to 15 May 1993,* ed. Linda Sharato (Ann Arbor, Mich.: Pierian Press, 1995), 190-1.

3.   David Royse, *Teaching Tips for College and University Instructors: A Practical Guide* (Boston: Allyn and Bacon, 2001), 158.

4.   Pederson, 190.

17

Miscellaneous

This chapter has a few brief topics along with sections on dealing with disruptive students, complaints in general, burnout, and teaching a credit course.

17.1
Put the library instruction right in the course textbook. This is great for home-grown texts (that may be professionally published). Have a copy of the library tour and an entire chapter on library research in a first-year composition book.

17.2
If there is going to be a large group in the library, or an assignment that requires the use of unusual resources, inform colleagues in advance about it. You might even keep copies of the assignment and lists of recommended sources at the reference desk (in print, electronic format, or both).

17.3
Hire librarians who enjoy teaching. Someone who actively dislikes it will either refuse to help out or will give off-putting presentations.

17.4
Offer in-house training for library instruction. Give workshops and also find time to discuss instructional ideas and concerns in more general library meetings.

17.5

Your technical service librarians may have great training ideas. Other library departments need to train their new staff on library procedures and databases too. Invite all library staff to join instruction improvement sessions.

17.6

Homographs to use as examples: gum (chewing, teeth holder), seal (animal, envelope closure, ring), neat (nifty, without water, tidy), cool (temperature, nifty), Venus (planet, goddess), Mercury (car, chemical, god, planet), Mars (god, planet), Saturn (car, planet, god), Milky Way (galaxy, candy bar), moon (crude display, satellite), satellite (moon, campus), lead (in front, metal), bow (arrow, courtesy, ribbon arrangement), train (railway, teach), program (TV show, handout at play/concert, something done with a computer), iris (eye, flower).

Homophones: bow, bough; so, sew, sow; flour, flower; some, sum; base, bass; knight, night; boy, buoy; maid, made; for, four, fore; great, grate; be, bee; meet, meat; missed, mist; tale, tail; wait, weight; knew, new, gnu; mail, male; or, oar; sale, sail; lie, lye; dye, die; know, no; week, weak; sight, site; rode, road, rowed; seen, scene; pail, pale; war, wore; bare, bear; son, sun; stare, stair; see, sea; days, daze; our, hour; one, won; brake, break; piece, peace; there, their, they're; sore, soar; stationary, stationery; wood, would; heel, heal; warn, worn; steal, steel; threw, through; groan, grown; weigh, way; here, hear; weather, whether; whine, wine.

Disruptive Students

17.7

Do not take disruptive behavior personally. The student who misbehaves in your session is probably a problem in the regular instructor's classroom too.

17.8

I do not consider it disruptive when students share a quick comment with one another. Brief side conversations reinforce a lesson or idea. A neighboring student can quickly point out a place on the screen.

17.9

State your classroom policies at the beginning of the session. Ask for quiet while you are talking so everyone can hear. State the policies in as positive a manner as you can.

17.10

A good instructor will ask his or her students to behave. The instructor will emphasize the importance of the library skills you are teaching for the successful completion of their assignment.

17.11

If students are talking, stop talking and wait for them to be quiet. Just stand there patiently. Usually the group will self-regulate—classmates will ask the talkers to be silent.

17.12

Walk over and stand next to the student who is disrupting class. Keep you eye on him or her. Most of the time the student does not want all the attention.

17.13

If two students are having their own private (but disruptive) conversation, ask them if they would like to leave the room to continue it.

17.14

Ask the talkers to share their conversation with the entire class. However, only do this if you are willing to hear public criticism of your teaching or other deliberately provocative remarks.

17.15

Invite anyone who wishes to leave to leave. This strategy is applicable only with older students. You probably should not have very young students wandering around your building unattended.

Complaints/Problems

17.16

Listen carefully to any complaints. Establish what the real problem is. It may be different from what the person is saying. Offer possible solutions. These may need to be worked out after class.

17.17

A library comment/suggestion box whether physical or online is a useful place where you can refer users with a complaint.

17.18

Stay calm when facing angry people. If you get upset you will only elevate a difficult situation.

17.19
Acknowledge that you are aware that the other person has a problem.

17.20
"Don't disagree with a person—only ideas of views. 'I don't think this would work in practice' is a diplomatic." way to respond to something far out. "Work hard at treating everyone equally."[1]

17.21
"Your listening skills may be your most valuable tool in any challenging situation. Really listening carefully to what is being said has several benefits. First it gives you the information you need to formulate an intelligent response. Second, it makes the patron feel respected and connected."[2]

17.22
Make sure you have heard the entire complaint or list of complaints before responding. The solution may be different when a problem is part of a number of problems.

17.23
You will need to remove physical distractions (noise). You may need to go to another part of the library to do this. Finding a place where you can really listen shows the person that you are really concerned about what he or she has to say.

17.24
Look at the person when he or she is talking and listen not only to what is being said verbally, but what is not being said. Watch the person's body language to see if something else might be going on.

17.25
Pay attention to what the person is saying—not to how he or she is dressed or speaking.

17.26
"Never make the person feel trapped or threatened. . . .

"Sitting down when talking to someone who is sitting down seems less threatening. If the person is standing, sit and invite them to sit. It's friendly, professional, and actually safer for you because it's harder to launch a physical attack when sitting, especially across a table. Don't stand between the person and the exit."[3]

17.27
Respond in a positive manner. Do not act as if the concern is silly or unimportant. It is important to that person right now.

17.28
If you are teaching a class session and someone has a list of complaints about the library, offer to listen to them after the session (and then listen—set up an appointment, if necessary).

17.29
Kitty Smith, *Serving the Difficult Customer A How-to-Do-It Manual for Library Staff*. How-to-Do-It Manuals for Libraries 39 (New York: Neal-Schuman, 1993) has many useful ideas. Pages 84-6 have specific useful strategies for listening to complaints.

17.30
Make sure that you follow through with any agreed solutions to a problem.

Burnout

17.31
Burnout is a disagreeable reality for some instruction librarians. It can be tiresome to repeat the same course lecture over and over to what can be disengaged students. If your equipment is constantly on the blink your frustration level will be higher.

17.32
Repetition tied to instruction also occurs outside the classroom. Dealing with scheduling can be a burden. If you have to telephone someone, or walk somewhere else, or deal with an annoying computer program every time you need to find out if a classroom is available, your stress levels will increase. Try to get the easiest possible system so you do not need to call instructors back (and risk them being away) when they want to schedule a session.

17.33
Coping with the details is another source of frustration. Is reporting your attendance numbers cumbersome? Is the key to the room kept somewhere inconvenient? A colleague who never returns the key and/or never leaves the board clean? Some annoyances are more difficult to cope with than others, so tackle the big ones first if you can.

17.34

Make every effort to eliminate the small annoyances. They add up. If your library is unable or unwilling to make things easier for you, the problem may be a flagrant lack of administrative support for your instruction program. Sometimes changing jobs is the only way out. Unfortunately, this is not an option for everyone. Reduce your teaching load (for example, do not advertise) if you can. In a bad situation it is better to do a few sessions well than many poorly.

17.35

"Accept the right to feel stressed. Don't pretend it's something that should never happen to you, or that it's a weakness on your part."[4]

17.36

"Teaching multiple sections of library instruction one-shot sessions to first-year students can cause symptoms of stress and burnout in the teaching librarian, symptoms that are remarkably similar to those experienced by helping professionals. These symptoms include:
- Cynicism and pessimism
- Greater concern with self and impersonal treatment of others
- A loss of one's 'center'
- Emotional exhaustion, numbness, depression, anxiety, and lack of enthusiasm
- Self-blame and feelings of reduced personal accomplishment"[5]

17.37

Suggested ways to combat stress and burnout:
- "Challenge yourself by using dynamic personal, and engaging instruction techniques, which make for a more stimulated and engaged instructor, as well as the students. . . .
- Build on what students already know and do not be afraid of making a fool of yourself to make a point and get their attention. . . .
- Remember to set goals first and keep them in focus when planning information literacy programs."[6]

17.38

If teaching the same course over and over:
- Change the sequence of your outline.
- Have an all Q & A session.
- Have students design the outline of the session.
- Hand out slips of paper to students and call on them. Request that they tell you the concept or idea listed and teach the session in that sequence.

17.39

Change your examples for each session without testing them first. The unexpected results will challenge you to make a recovery. This should make things more interesting for you.

17.40

Do examples from your own research. See what you can find on your topic in the indexes useful for your students' assignments. This can be a great teaching idea, because unless your research closely matches the students' topics, you will get few results. This can be used as examples of why it is important to find the best resources for a given topic. Or pick an outrageous topic that gets either good or bad results. (Be age appropriate.)

17.41

"Personal characteristics of BI librarians that may promote burnout include idealism, overdedication, and the setting of unrealistic goals. Bibliographic instruction is considered among the human service professions, and BI librarians do 'people work,' which is known to promote burnout. . . . Troublesome properties common to the BI scenario include insufficient staff, trying to cover too much material, only seeing a negative aspect of students' lives, little feedback from students, new librarians often carrying the responsibility for BI (remember that burnout primarily affects new professionals), feelings of little real impact on students' lives, too many classes, too many competing duties, tedious and repetitive course content, lack of proper training, lack of intellectual stimulation, and facing student apathy or resentment."[7]

17.42

"Numerous studies suggest that burnout potential is found both in the work environment and in individuals. Within the work environment, the most common stressors promoting burnout include decreased autonomy, role conflict, and role ambiguity. Decreased opportunities for personal accomplishment and inadequate positive feedback are also factors that promote burnout. Lack of control over system operations, no-win situations, continuously heavy workloads, and other physical stressors in the work environment correlated highly with the probability of burnout. Personal characteristics that increase susceptibility to burnout include high ideals, a tendency to overcommit oneself, and single-mindedness. Sex role stereotypes, experiences of sexism, age (young), education (college degree), and hours of employment (full time) were also identified as factors that could contribute to burnout."[8]

17.43

Janette S. Caputo's *Stress and Burnout in Library Service* (Phoenix, Ariz.: Oryx Press, 1991) has some useful charts with questions to evaluate the probability of burnout:

- Personal Burnout Quotient (pages 79-80)
- Job Burnout Quotient (pages 82-4)

There are also checklists for symptoms of physiological arousal, emotional exhaustion, mental exhaustion, complaints from family and friends, and complaints at work (pages 87, 93, 98, 103, and 105).

17.44

Attending workshops on teaching techniques can be a reinvigorating experience that can head off burnout.

17.45

Talk with colleagues about their experiences in the classroom. What techniques do they use to keep things interesting?

17.46

"Team teaching, methods that foster collaborative learning, and workshops in which BI librarians discuss approaches and techniques can be effective hedges against burnout. . . . In a workshop, BI librarians can share success stories that allow others to 're-vision' instruction in fresh new ways."[9]

17.47

Vary your instructional activities to fight burnout.

- "Teaching collaboratively with colleagues and teaching faculty, and observing each other's classes occasionally, can help to counteract stress and burnout. . . .
- The teaching librarian should not be afraid to 'make a fool of himself' to a degree to make a point more memorable. . . .
- The teaching librarian should strive for sessions one might characterize as 'controlled spontaneity.' As he or she becomes more comfortable and experienced teaching, sample topics for database searches, for example, can be solicited from the students."[10]

17.48

Be realistic about what you can accomplish in the classroom. Setting lofty goals that you will never reach will only increase your stress levels.

17.49

Be a student yourself. Taking classes (credit, non-credit, or workshop) are productive ways to learn new material and get new teaching ideas.

17.50
Repeating sessions might be reshaped as Web pages, online tutorials, or videos. Design these in conjunction with instructors who teach the course. Once completed, refer instructors to these resources. Offer to demonstrate how you would use the Web pages to the instructors. In online tutorials, build in quizzing features where responses can be automatically e-mailed to the course instructors.

Teaching a Credit Course

17.51
Make clear goals and objectives.

17.52
First day—fill out 3 x 5" cards or have the first assignment requesting students to e-mail information to you about their library experiences, expectations for the course, and academic and personal interests. The e-mail assignment proves that they have an e-mail account. Give credit for this note. Integrate student interests into the examples you show over the weeks of the course.

17.53
Ask students about work, religious obligations, a previous class on the other side of campus, etc. that might interfere with prompt class attendance or presence on certain dates.

17.54
Write changes to the syllabus dates on the board to be sure that newly arrived international students understand the change.[11] This is also helpful for English speakers with learning style differences.

17.55
Define what constitutes success in the course. Be clear about expected writing and other skills you will be grading.

17.56
Learning outcomes should be measurable. List them on the syllabus. For example, by the end of this course a successful student:
- will be able to gather relevant materials on a given topic. This will be demonstrated by the resources chosen and the descriptions thereof in the annotated bibliography turned in at the end of the semester.

- will recognize the parts of bibliographic citations for books and articles. This will be demonstrated by successful completion of the identifying of missing citation parts assignment and complete citations in the final project.
- will be able to search the local online catalog and find complete bibliographic citations, call numbers, and locations for books and other resources. This will be demonstrated by successful completion of the hands-on online catalog assignment, which includes the identifying of five or more books on his or her topic.
- will be able to list resources following a standard bibliographic citation format (APA, MLA, Chicago, Turabian, CBE, etc.); this may be accomplished manually or via the use of a standard bibliographic software program such as Endnote or ProCite. This will be demonstrated by turning in accurate citations in the bibliographic citation assignment and in the final annotated bibliography project.

17.57

A statement of what you consider the essential heart of learning about the library should be included. For example, I include this statement when I teach credit library research courses (adapted from the American Library Association):

Information Literacy competencies can be addressed within the following major ability categories:

The ability to ACCESS information:

articulate information needs; construct effective search strategies;

select appropriate resources;

use efficient retrieval techniques; and

consider issues relating to access to information—privacy, copyright, preservation, censorship, electronic access, exponential growth, and issues yet to come.

The ability to EVALUATE information:

critically examine for veracity, authority, and bias; and judge the value and relevance of information.

The ability to SYNTHESIZE information:

comprehend meaning and interpret material;

integrate and organize effectively;

apply to problem solving and decision making; and

communicate information successfully.

17.58

Provide definitions for writing assignments right in the syllabus. For example, writing assignments will ask for:

- **ABSTRACT**: a brief (up to 6 sentences) non-evaluative summary of an article, book, or other information source.

- **ANNOTATION**: a brief (4-6 sentences) critical evaluation of an article, book, or other information source. An annotation can include commentary on the content, writing quality, organization, etc. of the source. Thus, if the writer of the annotation disagrees with the source he or she is able to say so. (A good annotation will say *why* and offer brief proofs as well.)
- **SUMMARY**: a non-evaluative retelling of a written document or event, which includes only the major or important points. In the case of written materials (such as journal articles), it is shorter than the original document. The information is relayed in the same sequence as the original source. To use the same terms or to paraphrase (restating the same information using different words) without attribution is a form of plagiarism. One way to avoid the appearance of plagiarism in a summary is to begin with words such as: "The article entitled 'Resources' by Jane Author discusses/reports/analyzes/critiques. . . ." A summary does not include the opinions of its author.

17.59
Grade assignments fairly. If you state your expectations clearly there is less chance that you will be challenged.

17.60
See pros and cons of different types of assignment/assessment choices on pages 41-86 in Race, *The Lecturer's Toolkit*.

17.61
An annotated bibliography makes an excellent final project. Earlier assignments that require students to identify encyclopedias, books, articles, government documents, Web sites, etc. can fall into the project. The project can be in print or on the Web.

17.62
Students may use you as a sounding board with regard to their personal lives. If you are uncomfortable with this, be sure that you are familiar with local counseling resources so you can refer your students to them.

17.63
Discuss acceptable classroom behavior (use of cell phones, reading of newspapers, etc.) and academic expectations on the first day of class. Have a copy of your classroom policy on the syllabus or in the class textbook.

17.64
Recommendation: do not add students to the course after it is one-eighth over. The students will not be able to catch up and you will lose a lot of your time

trying to help them catch up. (Personal experience: the highest grade a late add has earned is a "C" for the course.)

17.65
Here is an example library research course outline. Look at syllabi for similar courses on the Web and adapt your section to fit your institution and teaching goals.

Session 1
Introduction; overview of syllabus; what is research?; local library; searching the library catalog.

Session 2
Research strategy; reference works; universal library concepts; term project overview; topic selection.
After this session meet with instructor and get topic approval. Topics must be approved.

Session 3
LC Classification/Dewey Classification; *LCSH*; bibliographic styles (MLA, APA). WebCT.

Session 4
Evaluating books; searching the online catalog and state union catalog, Interlibrary Loan.

Session 5
Basic reference sources—encyclopedias and dictionaries; bibliographies; scholarly journals vs. popular magazines; primary vs. secondary sources.

Session 6
Evaluating articles; identifying articles in indexes—print, electronic.

Session 7
Searching indexes—Web; SuDoc classification.

Session 8
What is the Internet?; searching the Web; different search engines; evaluating Web pages. Fee vs. free resources.

Session 9
Boolean logic; Venn diagrams; truncation and proximity operators. Discuss assigned article; using microfilm and microfiche.

Session 10
Asking good reference questions—"well asked" and "poorly asked" examples (note: no such thing as a "stupid" question); term project overview; MLA style.

Session 11
Government documents—print and on the Web.

Session 12
Database similarities; biographical sources; group annotations—persuade rest of class to read/watch something.

Session 13
Term project outlines (presentations).

Session 14
Statistics; almanacs; identifying key journals in a field; researching current issues.

Session 15
Nifty Web sites; Web search engines; topics per class interests (Possible: book reviews; finding information on careers, grad school, buying cars, health, companies).

Session 16
Research Project due (40% of grade). Students share own favorite Web sites; information literacy. Catch up.

17.66
Example assignment:
   Choose an article that you will be using on your research project.
   Provide complete bibliographic citation information (journal name, volume, date, etc.) for the article in proper MLA style. Write a thoughtful annotation of this article in 4-6 sentences. The analyzing guide we have been using in class at http://lib.colostate.edu/howto/evaljrl.html should be your guide.

17.67
If using WebCT or Blackboard (or institution-grown program) for some of your assignments, give instructions in your syllabus or in your textbook for it and explain how assignments or quizzes fit into the grading scheme. For example:

Select parts of your homework assignments are via WebCT. See your syllabus for when these are due, although statements made by me in class override anything written. These assignments must be finished before class time the day they are due. The program will not allow you to do an assignment late.

Even though WebCT calls your assignments "Quizzes," they are not considered quizzes by me. You are given two chances for each (one assignment, four chances); these are not intended to take very long (fewer than 20 minutes). However, you will want to **think about the assignments** (attending class and studying appropriate Web pages identified in class contribute to this) **before your first attempt** or the assignments will only bewilder you—they assume familiarity with library terms and concepts.

Answers will be provided at some point after the assignment is due. Grades should be available immediately. If you choose to redo an assignment, you will receive the highest grade. A redone assignment might not have the same questions as the earlier one.

If you have difficulty with the format of the WebCT quizzes (go through the sample assignment component to find this out), please see me as soon as possible so we can discuss alternative ways for you to complete the assignments. [A statement like this might not belong on an all-online course, but I have had traditional section students who had visual difficulties with WebCT assignments.]

17.68
Teach the course in the way that makes you the most comfortable. Do not force yourself to have group tasks or online activities if you are not comfortable with them.

17.69
Add or change topics and methods as needed. You will need to demonstrate the latest library databases, but your methods for teaching can evolve more slowly. If you want to try a new technique, see how it works out during an early week of the semester before completely changing over. It is more important for your students to learn the content than for you to use them as teaching experiments.

17.70
Have fun! It can be enjoyable to watch students increase their understanding of library research as the semester progresses.

Notes

1. Phil Race and Brenda Smith, *500 Tips for Trainers* (Houston, Tex.: Gulf, 1996), 97.

2. Mark R. Willis, *Dealing with Difficult People in the Library* (Chicago: American Library Association, 1999): 12.

3. Willis, 34.

4. Sally Brown, Bill Downey, and Phil Race, *500 Tips for Academic Librarians* (London: Library Association Publishing, 1997), 127.

5. Deborah F. Sheesley, moderator, "The One-Shot Multiple Section Freshman Instruction Session: Keeping the Teaching Librarian Stress-Free and Intellectually Stimulted," in *First Impressions, Lasting Impact: Introducing the First-Year Student to the Academic Library: Papers Presented at the Twenty-eighth National LOEX Library Instruction Conference held in Ypsilanti, Michigan, 19 to 20 May 2000*, ed. Julia K. Dims (Ann Arbor, Mich.: Pierian Press, 2002), 153.

6. Sheesley, "One Shot," 153-4.

7. Karen A. Becker, "The Characteristics of Bibliographic Instruction in Relation to the Causes and Symptoms of Burnout," *RQ* 32, no. 3 (1993): 355.

8. Janette S. Caputo, *Stress and Burnout in Library Service* (Phoenix, Ariz.: Oryx Press, 1991), 27.

9. Nancy Seale Osborne and Andrea Wyman, "The Forest and the Trees: A Modest Proposal on Bibliographic Burnout," *Research Strategies* 9 (1991): 103.

10. Deborah F. Sheesley, "Burnout and the Academic Teaching Librarian: An Examination of the Problem and Suggested Solutions," *The Journal of Academic Librarianship* 27 (2001): 449.

11. Debra S. Lee, "What Teachers Can Do to Relieve Problems Identified by International Students," in *Approaches to Teaching Non-Native English Speakers across the Curriculum*, New Directions for Teaching and Learning, no. 70, eds. David L. Sigsbee, Bruce W. Speck, and Bruce Maylath (San Francisco: Jossey-Bass, 1997), 95.

Appendix A

Example Syllabus 1

The Practical Approach

Course Objectives.
The successful Teaching Library Instruction student will have:

- experience with speaking in front of groups as demonstrated by having given five or more presentations on various topics to the entire class
- presented in more than one physical setup and/or location
- given a 50-minute presentation in front of two or three classmates
- demonstrated information-gathering skills in well-chosen and well-written annotated bibliography
- used critical thinking skills as demonstrated by thoughtful annotations in the annotated bibliography
- created outlines of presentations for actual courses or classes (syllabi from university or Web)
- created two or more electronic slide presentations with appropriate images that have only key terms and phrases, suitable for a traditional classroom setting
- created two or more electronic slide presentations with appropriate images that have only key terms and phrases, suitable for an online course
- created three instructional Web pages
- created two promotional flyers
- designed two workshops for a targeted audience
- observed and provided constructive feedback on classmate's teaching styles
- written two instructional goal statements
- designed hands-on assignments

Homework readings are from *Ideas for Librarians Who Teach*, unless otherwise specified.

Week 1

Introduction. Overview of syllabus. Three- to-five-minute introductions (length depends on number of students in class) of fellow students (after interviewing them). Knowing material. What should a librarian know before teaching a class about finding books, articles, and Web pages? What is a librarian trying to accomplish in the classroom? What is his or her role as guest lecturer? What can be realistically accomplished in a 50 (or 30)-minute session? What do students attending a required library instruction session expect from it?

    Homework: Read Chapters 1 & 2. Track down and read entire item from Notes in Chapter 2. Prepare to share additional tips with class. Select chapters/topics/books (and alternative choices) to present to class in week 6 and week 9, 10, 11, or 12 (two presentations).

Week 2

Librarian as key tool. Tips on speaking in front of groups. Discuss ideas from Chapter 2. Self-identify habit(s)/gesture(s) to immediately eliminate or add, based on introductory presentation first week of class. Practice standing comfortably and confidently in front of class (for five-ten minutes), while sharing tips from additional readings and favorite ideas from Chapter 2. Decide who will present which readings in week 6 and who and which in weeks 9, 10, 11, and 12.

    Homework: Read Chapter 3. Read through at least three of the "Useful Resources" listed in this chapter. Choose annotated bibliography topic and have it approved by instructor (instructor's choice of broad area: library science, information technology, education, and/or business).

Week 3

Customizing sessions. Discuss pros and cons of lectures, hands-on, group projects, etc. Discuss ACRL guidelines—what seems feasible? Too ambitions? How should learners' feelings throughout the stages of the search process be addressed? Answer questions on "Librarian Question Sheet" for hypothetical sessions (provided by instructor). Discuss how sessions might be crafted based on this.

    Homework: Read Chapter 4. Write measurable learning objectives for hypothetical sessions (described in class). Prepare two to three opening questions for the sessions. Prepare descriptions of the same research skill in two (or more) different ways (different skill for each student—establish a meaningful sequence). Read article (instructor's choice) and write a summary of it.

Week 4

In the classroom teaching. Getting over stage fright. Share opening questions with class from front of classroom. When asking questions look at class; class evaluates eye contact. Take turns teaching a research skill (two different ways— move to different part of room for second description) in meaningful sequence; class notes volume and vocal variation. (This emulates team teaching.) Evaluate the article summarized using "How to Evaluate a Journal Article" (http://lib.colostate.edu/howto/evaljrl.html) as a guide. Importance of critical thinking in library instruction—are existing evaluation tools useful for you? What would you include in an evaluation tool you might create?

Homework: Read Chapters 5 & 6. Students read information on different countries and their cultures in *CultureGrams* (based on student population at university). Skim Daniel Niemeyer, *Hard Facts on Smart Classroom Design: Ideas, Guidelines, and Layouts* (Lanham, Md.: Scarecrow Press, 2003) and Lisa Janiche Hinchliffe, *Neal-Schuman Electronic Classroom Handbook* (New York: Neal-Schuman, 2001). Prepare five-minute talk on assigned classroom-related topic (lighting, sound, space, etc.). Attend library instruction session as an observer.

Week 5

Diverse students. Discuss backgrounds of students on campus (may be rural vs. urban U.S. as well as international). Discuss local etiquette and behavior expectations of students and faculty. (This conversation should provide ideas about what students should ask colleagues when they get jobs elsewhere—even at a different library within the same community.) Useful discourse markers. Classroom. Describe pros and cons of room currently using. If movable tables and chairs, change the configuration and present prepared classroom topics (lighting, sound, space, tables, chairs, chalkboard, white board, floor, windows, temperature, location, etc.) in the different arrangement. If cannot change room, students present from different parts of the room to get a sense of how it feels to teach from a different location (and encourage comfort with different locations). Describe wish lists for new classrooms. Students make arrangements to meet for group homework assignment.

Homework: Students first write an outline for a talk (topic of choice; need not be library related; it is best that it is something with which the student is very familiar and knowledgeable—something that he or she can talk about for a full 50-minutes). Students make a commitment of 60 minutes times the number in the group (probably want at least three in the group, no more than four) to give an entire 50-minute lecture. This is done while standing (students who are unable to stand, because they use a wheelchair or have a health problem, present while sitting, but should fulfill the rest of the requirements). There is ten minutes—or longer if the group has time—for feedback. Timing, pacing, nerves, etc. can be discussed. Each member of the group should present, be given feedback, and see the others' presentations and give feedback. Preparation for class talk.

Week 6

Discussion on 50-minute talks. (Unless actually done, the amount of energy required to teach and the resulting exhaustion for an out-of-practice voice and body cannot be understood.) Presentations on Nancy Van Note Chism and Deborah J. Bickford, eds., *The Importance of Physical Space in Creating Supportive Learning Environments*, New Directions for Teaching and Learning, no. 92 (San Francisco: Jossey-Bass, 2002). There are ten chapters—assign as many students per chapter as divided by ten in the course—if there are nine students, the instructor can present one of them; fewer, assign two chapters per student and present as a team. Length of presentation depends on number of students in course. Create rough outline for talk to be prepared for homework.

Homework: Read Chapters 7 & 8. Prepare presentation software presentation #1 on topic of choice. Prepare section of assigned research talk and create two overhead transparencies for it (different sections of the topic for each student—topic could be finding literary criticism in books, tracking down primary sources, using preferred terms, evaluating books, finding a book on the shelf, etc.).

Week 7

Questions. Looking inviting. Take turns asking and answering. When to use visuals. Students present in sequence using their overheads. Discuss readability of different font styles and sizes. When would you use a flip chart? Presentation software? Overheads? Chalk/white board? Designing presentation software presentations. What to include, what not to include. How to format. Color. Number of lines. Images, audio, moving video. Being realistic about what you can do with real-life time constraints at work. Show parts of presentations from students and give feedback.

Homework: Read Chapters 9 & 10. Create instructional Web page #1. Identify 5-6 useful Web pages that could be linked to or used in the classroom on selected topic; describe why and when you would use them. Create presentation software presentation #2, suitable for first-year composition course (assignment from campus syllabus or from the Web) to be used in a classroom without live Internet connection. Create handout for class session—everyone in class does same topic (how to find an article, saving and e-mailing articles, or other topic), but chooses audience for it based on career interest (school, public, academic—4-year or community college, special, or corporate library).

Week 8

Using Web pages. What is or is not appropriate for different age groups? Access issues (vision, modem speed). Testing with users. What would you ask about your library's Web site? (For example, who is the subject librarian for history (academic site)? When is story hour for 3-year-olds (public library site)?) What topics are good candidates for online tutorials? Students present two of the Web pages they identified to the class—giving a description and evaluation of each. Class observes scrolling speed and how often the presenter is looking at them versus the screen. Pass around handouts and give feedback, as if members of chosen audience.

Homework: Create hands-on assignment for two different courses, as assigned by instructor. There should be at least twenty questions that are a combination of fill in the blank numbers (number of items owned) and fill in information (complete bibliographic citations or facts). Bring three copies to class—one for instructor, two for classmates to fill in and give feedback. Work on annotated bibliography.

Week 9

Presentations on sections of the National Cancer Institute, "Research-Based Web Design & Usability Guidelines." http://www.usability.gov/guidelines/index.html (or available equivalent). Presentation(s) on Newstrom, John W., and Edward Scannell, *The Big Book of Presentation Games: Wake-Em-Up Tricks, Ice Breakers, & Other Fun Stuff.* (New York: McGraw-Hill, 1998).

Homework: Read Chapters 11 & 12. Create instructional Web pages #2 and #3 on same topic for two distinct audiences (K-3, 4-6, 7-12, college, graduate student, members of a community). Advanced computer users might want to design brief online tutorials (again for specific audiences). Take MBTI test (subset available online or purchased).

Week 10

Humor in the classroom. Learning styles. Motivation. Different skills. Myers-Briggs Type Indicator and learning preferences. What would the classroom be like if every student were a North? South? East? West? What can you do to reach as many different students as is practicable? Communicating with people who are deaf or blind. (If available, invite guest who is deaf, with signing interpreter, if necessary, or blind, or from local disabled services to describe ways to communicate with people with disabilities.)

Homework: Read Chapter 13. Read *500 Tips on Group Learning* (Race). Write group learning exercise. Complete two classmates' hands-on assignments and comment on clarity of directions for completing them.

Week 11

Group learning. When to use it? Forming groups. Present preparations for group exercises. Use group methods to describe different methods. Discuss pros and cons of each. Cultural and gender concerns. Problems with group work. Presentation(s) on Green, Timothy D., "Responding and Sharing: Techniques for Energizing Classroom Discussions" (*Clearing House,* July/August 2000): 331-4, and Sutherland, Tracey E., and Charles C. Bonwell, eds., *Using Active Learning in College Classes: A Range of Options for Faculty,* New Directions for Teaching and Learning, no. 67 (San Francisco: Jossey-Bass, 1996). Presentation(s) on Berk, Ronald A. *Humor as an Instructional Defibrillator: Evidence-Based Techniques in Teaching and Assessment* (Sterling, Va.: Stylus, 2002).

Homework: Read Chapter 14. Create own evaluation form for class presentation. Videotape 15 to 30-minute presentation (if services available) and watch it. Work on annotated bibliography.

Week 12

Evaluation/feedback. Students give ten-minute presentations to class on research skill (can be the same one presented week 4 or 5). What good behaviors has the classmate shown? Does everyone have the seven good teaching traits (Arnold)? What could be improved? (Be gentle.) Classmates fill out evaluation form for each presenter (a good way to test the clarity of the questions). Presentation(s) on chapters from Ryan, Katherine E., ed., *Evaluating Teaching in Higher Education: A Vision for the Future,* New Directions for Teaching and Learning, no. 83 (San Francisco: Jossey-Bass, 2000) and Williams, Robin, *The Non-Designer's Design Book: Design and Typographic Principles for the Visual Novice,* 2nd ed. (Berkeley, Calif.: Peachpit Press, 2004).

Homework: Read Chapter 15. Design targeted flyer to post in specific departmental faculty mailroom or office that promotes library instruction services. After reading two different university or college mission statements (find both a large and a small school), write two library instruction mission statements that complement the institutions' (2-3 sentences). Draft two separate e-mail messages that promote workshops to a targeted audience on (1) searching the library catalog and (2) electronic indexes; include the subject line. Write outlines for the two workshops; include examples. Write hands-on exercises for these workshops.

Week 13

Promoting library instruction. How should you reach different constituents? Class designs a poster promoting the library for open school night at a K-6 school. Discuss mission statements and e-mails. Students present fifteen minutes of their workshops—either the beginning or the end.

Homework: Read Chapter 16. Create presentation software show suitable for online course on using the library from a distance. Topics are (1) identifying and acquiring articles (using at least two different vendors' electronic indexes), (2) evaluating what is found, and (3) citing the sources. Write library instruction guidelines for chosen career type library (school, public, academic—4-year or community college, special, or corporate). Who will you serve? How much preparation time do you require? What kinds of topics are you willing to cover? (Library research-only topics or production software too?)

Week 14
Distance education. How can a librarian be more involved? Difference between classroom and online presentation shows (e.g., single color backgrounds). Presentations left over from weeks 9, 10, 11, and 12.

  Homework: Read Chapter 17. Design flyer to post in young adult section of library that promotes summer reading. Design presentation software presentation suitable for online course. Topics are (1) searching the Web, (2) Boolean logic, and (3) truncation and proximity operators. Finalize annotated bibliography project.

Week 15
Turn in annotated bibliography. Dealing with complaints and problems. Avoiding burnout. Teaching a credit course. Other topics that arise which are of particular interest for students in this semester's course. Discuss or have students give short presentations on these topics. Is everyone now ready to teach? How will you describe your teaching skills in a cover letter and at a job interview?

Appendix B

Example Syllabus 2

The Theoretical Approach

Course Objectives.
The successful Teaching Library Instruction student will have:
- experience with speaking in front of groups as demonstrated by having given five or more presentations on various topics to the entire class
- presented in more than one physical setup and/or location
- given a 50-minute presentation on a learning theory in front of two or three classmates
- demonstrated information-gathering skills in well-chosen and well-written annotated bibliography
- used critical thinking skills as demonstrated by thoughtful annotations in the annotated bibliography
- created outlines of presentations for actual courses or classes (syllabi from university or Web)
- created an electronic slide presentation with appropriate images that has only key terms and phrases, suitable for a traditional classroom setting
- created an electronic slide presentation with appropriate images that has only key terms and phrases, suitable for an online course
- created an instructional Web page
- created a promotional flyer
- designed two workshops for a faculty audience
- observed and provided constructive feedback on classmate's teaching styles
- written an instructional program guideline for an academic library
- designed a hands-on assignment

Homework readings are from *Ideas for Librarians Who Teach*, unless otherwise specified. Full citations of other readings are found in the week the resource is discussed.

Week 1

Introduction. Overview of syllabus. Three to five minute introductions (length depends on number of students in class) of fellow students (after interviewing them). Read Chapter 1 of *Ideas*. Knowing material. What should a librarian know before teaching a class about finding books, articles, and Web pages? What is a librarian trying to accomplish in the classroom? What is his/her role as guest lecturer? What can be realistically accomplished in a 50 (or 30) minute session? What do students attending a required library instruction session expect from it?

Homework: Read Chapter 12. Read selections from *Principles of Instructional Design, What Every Teacher Should Know about Learning, Memory, and the Brain,* and *What Every Teacher Should Know about Instructional Planning.*

Week 2

Discuss learning styles, learning theories, and instructional planning as described in Chapter 12 and selections from Robert M. Gagné, Leslie J. Briggs, and Walter W. Wager, *Principles of Instructional Design*, 4th ed. (Fort Worth, Tex.: Harcourt Brace Jovanovich, 1992); Donna Walker Tileston, *What Every Teacher Should Know about Learning, Memory, and the Brain* (Thousand Oaks, Calif.: Corwin Press, 2004), and Donna Walker Tileston, *What Every Teacher Should Know about Instructional Planning* (Thousand Oaks, Calif.: Corwin Press, 2004).

Homework: Read Chapter 6. Read assigned chapter from *The Importance of Physical Space in Creating Supportive Learning Environments* and prepare presentation on it. Skim (or read instructor assigned pages from) *Student Learning in the Information Age* and *Seeking Meaning: A Process Approach to Library and Information Services.*

Weeks 3 and 4

Students present different chapters of Nancy Van Note Chism and Deborah J. Bickford, eds., *The Importance of Physical Space in Creating Supportive Learning Environments*, New Directions for Teaching and Learning, no. 92 (San Francisco: Jossey-Bass, 2002). Discuss readings from Patricia Senn Breivik. *Student Learning in the Information Age* (Phoenix, Ariz.: Oryx Press, 1998), and Carol C. Kuhthau. *Seeking Meaning: A Process Approach to Library and Information Services* (Norwood, N.J.: Ablex, 1993). Discuss pros and cons of course classroom.

Homework: Read Chapter 9. Go through "Research-Based Web Design & Usability Guidelines" Web site, read pages 9-11 and 63-4 of *Using the Myers-Briggs Type Indicator in Organizations: Workshop Leaders' Guide*, and assigned pages from *Information Literacy Instruction: Theory and Practice.* Choose annotated bibliography topic and have it approved by instructor (instructor's choice of broad area: library science, information technology, education, and/or business). Attend library instruction session as an observer.

Week 5

Discuss teaching ideas from Sandra Krebs Hirsh, *Using the Myers-Briggs Type Indicator in Organizations: Workshop Leaders' Guide,* 2nd ed. (Palo Alto, Calif.: Consulting Psychologists Press, 1991), Web site design concerns as described on National Cancer Institute, "Research-Based Web Design & Usability Guidelines" http://www.usability.gov/guidelines/index.htm, and Esther S. Grassian. *Information Literacy Instruction: Theory and Practice* (New York: Neal-Schuman, 2001).

Homework: Read Chapters 2, 5, and 13. Read *500 Tips on Group Learning.* Write group learning exercise. Read ACRL Guidelines for Instructional Programs in Academic Libraries, Information Literacy Competency Standards for Higher Education, Objectives for Information Literacy Instruction: A Model Statement for Academic Librarians; divide class reading among "Responding and Sharing: Techniques for Energizing Classroom Discussions," *Teaching at Its Best: A Research-Based Resource for College Instruction,* and James H. Stronge, *Qualities of Effective Teachers* (Alexandra, Va.: Association for Supervision and Curriculum Development, 2002),

Weeks 6 and 7

Presentations, discussion of Chapters 2, 5, 13, and ACRL Guidelines for Instructional Programs in Academic Libraries. June 2003. http://www.ala.org/ala/acrl/acrlstandards/guidelinesinstruction.htm; Association of College and Research Libraries (ACRL). Information Literacy Competency Standards for Higher Education. January 2000. PDF. http://www.ala.org/ala/acrl/acrlstandard/standards.pdf; Association of College and Research Libraries (ACRL). Objectives for Information Literacy Instruction: A Model Statement for Academic Librarians. June 2001. http://www.ala.org/ala/acrl/acrlstandards/objectivesinformation.htm; Timothy D. Green, "Responding and Sharing: Techniques for Energizing Classroom Discussions," *Clearing House,* July/August 2000: 331-4; Linda B. Nilson, *Teaching at Its Best: A Research-Based Resource for College Instruction* (Bolton, Mass.: Anker, 1998), and Phil Race, *500 Tips on Group Learning* (London: Kogan Page, 2000).

Homework: Read Chapter 14. Read assigned sections of *Evaluating Teachers for Professional Growth: Creating a Culture of Motivation and Learning, Peer Review of Teaching: A Sourcebook, Fresh Approaches to the*

Evaluation of Teaching, and *Evaluating Teaching in Higher Education: A Vision for the Future.*

Week 8

Presentations and discussion of assigned sections of Christopher Knapper and Patricia Cranton, eds., *Fresh Approaches to the Evaluation of Teaching,* New Directions for Teaching and Learning, no. 88 (San Francisco: Jossey-Bass, 2001), Katherine E. Ryan, ed., *Evaluating Teaching in Higher Education: A Vision for the Future,* New Directions for Teaching and Learning, no. 83 (San Francisco: Jossey-Bass, 2000), Daniel R. Beerens, *Evaluating Teachers for Professional Growth: Creating a Culture of Motivation and Learning* (Thousand Oaks, Calif.: Corwin Press, 2000), and Nancy Van Note Chism, *Peer Review of Teaching: A Sourcebook* (Bolton, Mass.: Anker, 1999). Assign three or four learning theories (discussed in week 2) to research in depth for 50-minute presentation. Students make arrangements to meet for group homework.

Homework: Do research and prepare outline for 50-minute presentation on assigned learning theory. Students make a commitment of 60 minutes times the number in the group (probably want at least three in the group, no more than four) to give an entire 50-minute lecture. This is done while standing (students who are unable to stand, because they use a wheelchair or have a health problem, present while sitting, but should fulfill the rest of the requirements). There is ten minutes—or longer if the group has time—for feedback. Timing, pacing, nerves, etc. can be discussed. Each member of the group should present, be given feedback, and to see the others' presentations and give feedback. Read Chapter 3.

Week 9

Discussion on 50-minute talks (unless actually done, the amount of energy required to teach and the resulting exhaustion for an out-of-practice voice and body cannot be understood) and learning theories. Catch up on first 8 weeks' topics and on customizing sessions. Assign research skill to teach.

Homework: Read Chapter 4. Prepare outline for teaching research skill in two different ways to a targeted audience in 15 minutes. Write evaluation form for same. Write library instruction guidelines for target chosen career type library (school, public, academic—4-year or community college, special, or corporate).

Week 10

Discussion of Chapter 4. Students present assigned research skill in meaningful sequence (informing class of targeted audience before start). Class gives feedback on eye contact, volume, and voice variation.

Homework: Read Chapters 7 and 8. Create presentation software presentation designed for first-year composition course in room without live Internet connection.

Week 11

Discussion of Chapters 7 and 8. Review of presentation programs; subset thereof presented to entire class. Feedback on same.

Homework: Read Chapters 10 and 11. Revise electronic presentation. Design two workshops and evaluation form for same for faculty audience on (1) searching the library catalog and (2) electronic indexes. Include examples. Create handout for class session—everyone in class does same topic (how to find an article, saving and e-mailing articles, or other topic), but chooses audience for it based on career interest (school, public, academic—4-year or community college, special, or corporate library).

Week 12

Meet in different classroom with different configuration or in classroom with the furniture rearranged. Present 15 minutes of workshop (beginning or end). Classmates fill out evaluation form. Discuss appropriate levels and amount of information for different audiences. Share handouts and give feedback as if members of targeted audience (K-6 might notice if there are no pictures).

Homework: Read Chapter 15 and Robin Williams, *The Non-Designer's Design Book: Design and Typographic Principles for the Visual Novice,* 2nd ed. (Berkeley, Calif.: Peachpit Press, 2004). Create promotional flyer for selected target audience on library instruction services. Create hands-on assignment for same audience (make four copies).

Week 13

Discussion on promoting library instruction. Class evaluates flyers and completes hands-on assignments. Look at and critique existing instructional Web pages.

Homework: Reread Chapter 9 and read Chapter 16. Read assigned chapter from *Teaching and Learning at a Distance: What It Takes to Effectively Design, Deliver, and Evaluate Programs.* Create subject-related Web page for targeted audience. Create presentation slide presentation suitable for online course. Topics are (1) identifying and acquiring articles (using at least two different vendor's electronic indexes), (2) evaluating what is found, and (3) citing the sources.

Week 14

Presentation of Web pages to class; presentation of presentation slides for online course. Discussion and feedback; does everyone demonstrate traits of effective teachers? Discussion of readings from Thomas E. Cyrs, *Teaching and Learning at a Distance: What It Takes to Effectively Design, Deliver, and Evaluate Programs*, New Directions for Teaching and Learning, no. 71 (San Francisco: Jossey-Bass, 1997).

Homework: Read Chapter 17. Finalize annotated bibliography.

Week 15
Turn in annotated bibliography. Dealing with complaints and problems. Avoiding burnout. Teaching a credit course. Other topics that arise which are of particular interest for students in this semester's course. Discuss or have students give short presentations on these topics. Is everyone now ready to teach? How will you describe your teaching skills in a cover letter and at a job interview?

Appendix C

Example Workshop Outline

Workshop Objectives.
Students completing the workshop will have:
- experience with speaking in front of a group
- presented in more than one physical setup and/or location
- participated in small group sharing exercises
- created outline of presentation for actual course (syllabi with assignment provided by workshop leader)
- created promotional flyer
- designed workshop for a targeted audience
- observed and provided constructive feedback on workshop participants' teaching styles

Readings are from *Ideas for Librarians Who Teach*. After the workshop, read the rest of the book and keep it in the office for future reference. Track down and read interesting articles, books, or Web pages cited in the book.

Time frame for each activity (for instance, some of the presentations can be extended to 20 minutes each) will depend upon whether the workshop is 4, 8, 12, or 16 hours long. (For a 12- or 16-hour workshop, additional topics, identified as of interest on day one, can be covered; specific ideas can be read from relevant chapters of the book in the evening between days; for a 4-hour workshop, parts will need to be cut.) Schedule breaks with snacks and drinks.

First part:
Introduction to workshop. Overview. Icebreaker (idea 4.80, customized). (Meeting people time.)

Assign one of three designations to attendees; a letter (used here: ABC) or name for each. They will be mixing with other participants throughout the workshop.

Second part:
After interviewing fellow attendee, give two-minute introduction of same to entire group; participants give introductions standing in different parts of the room. (First chance to address the group as a whole.)

Third part:
Everyone reads Chapter 1. (Quiet time.)
Discussion on knowing material. What should a librarian know before teaching a class about finding books, articles, and Web pages? What is a librarian trying to accomplish in the classroom? What is his or her role as guest lecturer? What can be realistically accomplished in a 50 (or 30)-minute session? What do college students attending a required library instruction session expect from it? What do community members expect from a public library session? From story hour?

Fourth part:
A's read ideas 2.1-2.25; B's ideas 2.26-2.48; C's ideas 2.49-2.72. (Quiet time.)
Groups of three to five with A, B, and C readers meet and share ideas from the book. (Talking, sharing time.)

Fifth part:
Everyone reads ideas 3.1-3.2; 3.24-3.27; 3.45; 3.50-3.53; 4.1-4.16; 4.21; 4.27-4.29; 4.53; 4.67; 4.70; 4.76-4.77; 5.21-5.22. (Quiet time.)
1) Self-identify habit(s)/gesture(s) to immediately eliminate or add, based on introductory presentation.
2) Write two opening questions for targeted audience.

Sixth part:
Discuss being in the classroom teaching. Getting over stage fright.
Everyone shares opening questions with class from front of classroom (first informing attendees who the targeted audience is). When asking questions look at group; group evaluates eye contact.

Seventh part:
Research skill to teach group is chosen/assigned to pairs/groups (provided by workshop leader).
Two or three participants prepare teaching outline for designated research skill. Each member of the group will present for five minutes. Discuss

approaches and presentation skills to work on. (Pair or group of three people time.)

Eighth part:
Read 6.1-6.11; 7.1-7.27. (Quiet time.)

Ninth part:
Everyone teaches own section of assigned research skill to entire group. Group notes volume and vocal variation. (Team teaching; speaking in front of group.) Group asks questions for clarification. (Q&A experience.)

Tenth part:
Discussion on classroom arrangements. Describe pros and cons of room currently using. If movable tables and chairs, change the configuration of the room. (Entire group.)

Eleventh part:
Discussion on inviting questions. (Entire group.)
    Take turns asking and answering questions (learn research tips from other participants) in new ABC groups. (Small group participation.)

Twelfth part:
Read 8.2-8.9; 8.25-8.40; 8.44-8.49; 8.57-8.60; 8.76; 8.81-8.92. (Quiet time.)
    Discuss when to use visuals. When would you use a flip chart? Presentation software? Overheads? Chalk/white board? Designing presentation software presentations. What to include, what not to include. How to format. Color. Number of lines. Images, audio, moving video. Being realistic about what you can do with real-life time constraints at work. (Entire group.)
    Design on paper (see 8.44) presentation software presentation to teach research skill presented earlier. (Quiet time.)
    Share and get feedback from new ABC group. (Small group participation.)

Thirteenth part:
Read 9.15-9.22; 9.28-9.32. (Quiet time.)
    Discuss using Web pages. What is or is not appropriate for different age groups? Access issues (vision, modem speed). Testing with users. What would you ask about your library's Web site? [For example: Who is the subject librarian for history (academic site)? When is story hour for 3-year-olds (public library site)?] (Entire group.)

Fourteenth part:
Read 10.2-10.13; 10.26-10.29; 11.1-11.13; 11.18; 11.20; 11.24; 12.1-12.5; 12.36. (Quiet time.)

Discuss use of handouts and humor in the classroom. Discuss learning styles. (Entire group.)

Fifteenth part:
Read 13.1-13.4; 13.11; 13.17-13.20. (Quiet time.)
    Group learning. When to use it? Forming groups. Come up with other ways to form groups. (Entire group.)

Sixteenth part:
Workshop leader provides syllabus with assigned topic to each participant.
    Read 14.5; 14.8; 14.12-14.14; 14.21. Each participant prepares presentation to prepare students to complete their assignment. (Quiet time.)
    Discuss evaluation and feedback. Behaviors to observe. (Entire group.)
    Participants give ten-minute presentations to class on assigned topic. What good behaviors has the participant shown? What could be improved? (Be gentle.) Participants fill out evaluation form for each presenter. Use questions from *Ideas* (14.21) to evaluate presentations.

Seventeenth part:
Write outline for workshop to a targeted audience on searching the library catalog. (Quiet time.)
    Participants present fifteen minutes of their workshops—either the beginning or the end. (Entire group.)

Eighteenth part:
Read 15.2-15.3; 15.29; 15.40.
    Discuss promoting library instruction. How should you reach different constituents? Group designs a poster promoting the library for open school night at a K-6 school. Participants design poster that highlights what was learned during the workshop. (Entire group.)
    Workshop evaluation.

Bibliography

Aguilar, Leslie, and Linda Stokes. *Multicultural Customer Service: Providing Outstanding Service Across Cultures.* Business Skills Express Series. N.p.: Irwin Professional, 1996.

Alberico, Ralph, and Elizabeth A. Dupuis. "The World Wide Web as an Instructional Medium." in *New Ways of "Learning the Library"—and Beyond: Papers and Sessions Material Presented at the Twenty-third National LOEX Library Instruction Conference Held in Denton, Texas, 5 to 6 May 1995.* ed. Linda Shirato, Elizabeth R. Bucciarelli, and Heidi Mercado, 27-36. Ann Arbor, Mich.: Pierian Press, 1996.

American Association of School Librarians. Position Statement on Resource Based Instruction: Role of the School Library Media Specialist in Reading Development. http://www.ala.org/ala/aasl/aaslproftools/positionstatements/aaslpositionstatementre source.htm (accessed May 16, 2004).

Anderson, David, Sally Brown, and Phil Race. *500 Tips for Further and Continuing Education Lecturers.* London: Kogan Page, 1998.

Anderson, Karrin. *Speech Coursebook.* N.p.: Thomson Custom Publishing, 2003.

Anthony, Ray. *Talking to the Top: Executive's Guide to Career-Making Presentations.* Englewood Cliffs, N.J.: Prentice Hall, 1995.

Arnold, Judith M. "I Know It When I See It: Assessing Good Teaching," *Research Strategies* 16, no. 1 (1998): 1-28.

Association of College and Research Libraries (ACRL). Guidelines for Instructional Programs in Academic Libraries. June 2003. http://www.ala.org/ala/acrl/ acrlstandards/guidelinesinstruction.htm (accessed May 16, 2004).

———. Information Literacy Competency Standards for Higher Education. January 2000. PDF. http://www.ala.org/ala/acrl/acrlstandard/standards.pdf (accessed May 16, 2004).

———. Objectives for Information Literacy Instruction: A Model Statement for Academic Librarians. June 2001. http://www.ala.org/ala/acrl/acrlstandards/ objectivesinformation.htm (accessed May 16, 2004).

Axtell, Roger E., ed. *Do's and Taboos Around the World.* 3rd ed. New York: Benjamin, 1993.

Ballard, Brigid, and John Clanchy. *Teaching International Students: A Brief Guide for Lecturers and Supervisors.* Deakin, ACT, Australia: IDP Education Australia, 1997.

Baule, Steven M., and Laura Blair Bertani. "How to Gain Support from Your Board and Administrators: Marketing 101 for Your Library Media Program." *Book Report,* November/December 2000: 47-9.

Becker, Karen A. "The Characteristics of Bibliographic Instruction in Relation to the Causes and Symptoms of Burnout." *RQ* 32, no. 3 (1993): 346-57.

Beerens, Daniel R. *Evaluating Teachers for Professional Growth: Creating a Culture of Motivation and Learning.* Thousand Oaks, Calif.: Corwin Press, 2000.

Berk, Ronald A. *Humor as an Instructional Defibrillator: Evidence-Based Techniques in Teaching and Assessment.* Sterling, Va.: Stylus, 2002.

———. *Professors Are from Mars®, Students Are from Snickers®: How to Write and Deliver Humor in the Classroom and in Professional Presentations.* Sterling, Va.: Stylus, 2003.

Bethel, William. *10 Steps to Connecting with Your Customers.* Chicago, Ill.: Dartnell Press, 1995.

Bickford, Deborah J. "Navigating the White Waters of Collaborative Work in Shaping Learning Environments." In *The Importance of Physical Space in Creating Supportive Learning Environments,* New Directions for Teaching and Learning, no. 92, edited by Nancy Van Note Chism and Deborah J. Bickford, 43-52. San Francisco: Jossey-Bass, 2002.

Biggs, John. *Teaching for Quality Learning at University,* 2nd ed. The Society for Research into Higher Education. Buckingham [England]: Open University Press, 2003.

Bobby™. http://bobby.watchfire.com/bobby/html/en/index.jsp (accessed May 24, 2004).

Bodi, Sonia. "Scholarship or Propaganda: How Can Librarians Help Undergraduates Tell the Difference?" *Journal of Academic Librarianship* 21 (1995): 21-5.

Bonwell, Charles C. "Enhancing the Lecture: Revitalizing a Traditional Format." In *Using Active Learning in College Classes: A Range of Options for Faculty,* New Directions for Teaching and Learning, no. 67, edited by Tracey E. Sutherland and Charles C. Bonwell. San Francisco: Jossey-Bass, 1996. 31-44.

Brace, Patricia, Rick Gordon, and Elizabeth Schumaker. *Writing & Students with Special Needs: A Manual for Writing Centre Tutors.* Kingston, Ontario: Queen's University, 1994.

Breivik, Patricia Senn. *Planning the Library Instruction Program.* Chicago: American Library Association, 1982.

———. *Student Learning in the Information Age.* Phoenix, Ariz.: Oryx Press, 1998.

Brinkley, Alan, et al. *The Chicago Handbook for Teachers: A Practical Guide to the College Classroom.* Chicago: University of Chicago Press, 1999.

Brisco, Shonda. "From Braille to Zoom Text: Resources to Meet the Needs of Blind or Visually Impaired Students in the Media Center." *Library Media Connection,* August/September 2003: 50-3.

Brottman, May, and Mary Loe, eds. *The LIRT Library Instruction Handbook.* Englewood, Colo.: Libraries Unlimited, 1990.

Brown, Sally, Bill Downey, and Phil Race. *500 Tips for Academic Librarians.* London: Library Association Publishing, 1997.

Browne, M. Neil, and Kari Freeman. "Distinguishing Features of Critical Thinking Classrooms." *Teaching in Higher Education* 5, no. 3 (2000): 301-9.

Caputo, Janette S. *Stress and Burnout in Library Service.* Phoenix, Ariz.: Oryx Press, 1991.

Carbone, Elisa. *Teaching Large Classes: Tools and Strategies.* Survival Skills for Scholars, vol. 19. Thousand Oaks, Calif.: Sage Publications, 1998.

Carter, Elizabeth W. "'Doing the Best You Can with What You Have:' Lessons Learned from Outcomes Assessment." *Journal of Academic Librarianship* 28, no. 1 (2002): 36-41.

Case, Roland. "Making Critical Thinking an Integral Part of Electronic Research." *School Libraries in Canada* 22, no. 4 (2003): 13-16.

Chism, Nancy Van Note. *Peer Review of Teaching: A Sourcebook.* Bolton, Mass.: Anker, 1999.

Chism, Nancy Van Note, and Deborah J. Bickford, eds. *The Importance of Physical Space in Creating Supportive Learning Environments,* New Directions for Teaching and Learning, no. 92. San Francisco: Jossey-Bass, 2002.

Cornelio, Alicia. "Promoting Information Literacy through Information Architecture." *Library Media Connection,* March 2003: 24-6.

Cornell, Paul. "The Impact of Changes in Teaching and Learning on Furniture and the Learning Environment." In *The Importance of Physical Space in Creating Supportive Learning Environments,* New Directions for Teaching and Learning, no. 92, edited by Nancy Van Note Chism and Deborah J. Bickford, 33-42. San Francisco: Jossey-Bass, 2002.

CultureGrams. Lindon, Utah: Axiom Press, annual.

Cyrs, Thomas C. "Visual Thinking: Let Them See What You Are Saying." In *Teaching and Learning at a Distance: What It Takes to Effectively Design, Deliver and Evaluate Programs,* New Directions for Teaching and Learning, no. 71, edited by Thomas C. Cyrs, 27-32. San Francisco: Jossey-Bass, 1997.

Cyrs, Thomas C. ed. *Teaching and Learning at a Distance: What It Takes to Effectively Design, Deliver and Evaluate Programs,* New Directions for Teaching and Learning, no. 71. San Francisco: Jossey-Bass, 1997.

Dahl, Katherine. "The Politics of Book Reviews: Or, It's Hard to Say Something Nice When You're Ideologically or Philosophically Indisposed Toward Doing So," In *Judging the Validity of Information Sources: Teaching Critical Analysis Bibliographic Instruction: Papers and Session Materials Presented at the Eighteenth National LOEX Library Instruction Conference Held at Eastern Michigan University, 11 to 12 May 1990, and Related Resource Materials Gathered by the LOEX Clearinghouse,* edited by Linda Shirato, 49-56. Ann Arbor, Mich.: Pierian Press, 1991.

Deines-Jones, Courtney, and Connie Van Fleet. *Preparing Staff to Serve Patrons with Disabilities: A How-to-Do-It Manual.* How-to-Do-It Manuals for Librarians 57. New York: Neal-Schuman, 1995.

Doctor HTML. http://www2.imagiware.com/RxHTML/ (accessed May 14, 2005)

Dunn, Rita. "Introduction to Learning Styles." In *The Complete Guide to the Learning Styles Inservice System,* Rita Dunn and Kenneth Dunn, 11-29. Boston: Allyn and Bacon, 1999.

———. *Strategies for Educating Diverse Learners.* FASTBACK® 384. Bloomington, Ind.: Phi Delta Kappa Educational Foundation, 1995.

Dworkin, Kristine D. "Library Marketing: Eight Ways to Get Unconventionally Creative." *Online,* January/February 2001: 54.

Ehrenborg, Jöns, and John Mattock. *Powerful Presentations: Simple Ideas for Making a Real Impact.* 2nd ed. London: Kogan Page, 1997.

Elsea, Janet G. *The Four-Minute Sell.* New York: Simon and Schuster, 1984.

Emerson, Zara, ed. *About Face: Reviving the Rules of Typography.* Mies, Switzerland: RotoVision, 2002.

Ferguson, Douglas. "Marketing Online Services in the University." *Online* 1, no. 3 (1977): 15-23.

Foster, Susan. *Smart Packing for Today's Traveler.* Portland, Ore.: Smart Travel Press, 2000.

Frick, Elizabeth. "Theories of Learning and Their Impact on OPAC Instruction." *Research Strategies* 7, no. 2 (1989): 68-9.

Gagné, Robert M., Leslie J. Briggs, and Walter W. Wager. *Principles of Instructional Design.* 4th ed. Australia: Wadsworth Thomson Learning, 1992.

Gee, Gordon E., and Patricia Senn Breivik. "Libraries and Learning." In *Libraries and the Search for Academic Excellence. Proceedings of the Arden House Symposium.* New York, NY; March 15-17, 1987. See IR 052 055. ERIC ED 284 593.

Gesteland, Richard R. *Cross-Cultural Business Behavior: Marketing, Negotiating, Sourcing and Managing Cross Cultures.* 3rd ed. Copenhagen, Denmark: Copenhagen Business School Press, 2002.

Grassian, Esther S. *Information Literacy Instruction: Theory and Practice.* New York: Neal-Schuman, 2001.

Green, Timothy D. "Responding and Sharing: Techniques for Energizing Classroom Discussions." *Clearing House,* July/August 2000: 331-4.

Gribas, Cyndy, and Lynn Sykes. "Creating Great Overheads with Computers." *College Teaching* 44, no. 2 (1996): 66- [3 pages]. *Academic Search Premier*, Colorado State University Libraries. http://web8.epnet.com/ (accessed May 12, 2004).

Guest, Ross. "The Instructor's Optimal Mix of Teaching Methods." *Education Economics* 9, no. 3 (2001): 313-26.

Hanke, Jon. "The Psychology of Presentation Visuals." *Presentations,* May 1988: 42-51. *ABI/Inform,* Colorado State University Libraries. http://jake.prod.oclc.org:3055/ (accessed July 9, 1998).

Hardy, Darcy Walsh, and Mary H. Boaz. "Learner Development: Beyond the Technology." In *Teaching and Learning at a Distance: What it Takes to Effectively Design, Deliver and Evaluate Programs,* New Directions for Teaching and Learning, no. 71, edited by Thomas C. Cyrs, 41-8. San Francisco: Jossey-Bass, 1997.

Hill, Deborah J. *Humor in the Classroom: A Handbook for Teachers (and Other Entertainers!).* Springfield, Ill.: Charles C. Thomas, 1988.

Hinchliffe, Lisa Janiche. *Neal-Schuman Electronic Classroom Handbook.* New York: Neal-Schuman, 2001.

Hirsh, Sandra Krebs. *Using the Myers-Briggs Type Indicator in Organizations: Workshop Leaders' Guide.* 2nd ed. Palo Alto, Calif.: Consulting Psychologists Press, 1991.

Hobson, Mary K. "Helping Young Readers Find Their Favorite Book Characters and Subjects." *Library Media Connection,* February 2003: 12.

Hoener, Arthur,, Spencer Salend, and Sandra I. Kay. "Creating Readable Handouts, Worksheets, Overheads, Tests, Review Materials, Study Guides, and Homework Assignments Through Effective Typographic Design." *Teaching Exceptional Children,* January/February 1997: 32-5.

Hoff, Ron. *"I Can See You Naked": A Fearless Guide to Making Great Presentations.* Kansas City: Andrews and McMeel, 1988.

Holzschlag, Molly E. "Satisfying Customers with Color, Shape, and Type." *New Architect: Internet Strategies for Technology Leaders.* http://www.webtechniques. com/archives/1999/11desi/ (accessed May 16, 2004).

Johnson, Ellen. "Cultural Norms Affect Oral Communication in the Classroom." In *Approaches to Teaching Non-Native English Speakers across the Curriculum*, New Directions for Teaching and Learning, no. 70, edited by David L. Sigsbee, Bruce W. Speck, and Bruce Maylath, 47-52. San Francisco: Jossey-Bass, 1997.

Johnson, Virginia. "Picture-Perfect Presentations." *Training & Development Journal*, May 1989: 45-7.

Kalish, Karen. *How to Give a Terrific Presentation.* The WorkSmart Series. New York: Amacon, 1997.

Kilcullen, Maureen. "Teaching Librarians to Teach: Recommendations on What We Need to Know." *Reference Services Review* 26, no. 2 (1998): 7-18.

King, Jerry. "Laughter and Lesson Plans." *Techniques: Making Education and Career Connections*, January 1999: 34- [2 pages]. *Academic Search Premier*, Colorado State University Libraries. http://web8.epnet.com/ (accessed May 8, 2004).

Knapper, Christopher, and Patricia Cranton, eds., *Fresh Approaches to the Evaluation of Teaching*, New Directions for Teaching and Learning, no. 88. San Francisco: Jossey-Bass, 2001.

Kroenke, Kurt. "Handouts: Making the Lecture Portable." *Medical Teacher* 13, no. 3 (1991): 199- [5 pages]. *Academic Search Premier*, Colorado State University Libraries. http://web8.epnet.com/ (accessed May 8, 2004).

Kuhlthau, Carol C. "Information Skills for an Information Society: A Review of Research: An ERIC Information Analysis Product." ED 297 740. Syracuse, NY: ERIC, 1987.

———. "The Process Approach to Bibliographic Instruction: An Examination of the Search Process in Preparation for Writing the Research Paper." In *Judging the Validity of Information Sources: Teaching Critical Analysis Bibliographic Instruction: Papers and Session Materials Presented at the Eighteenth National LOEX Library Instruction Conference Held at Eastern Michigan University, 11 to 12 May 1990, and Related Resource Materials Gathered by the LOEX Clearinghouse*, edited by Linda Shirato, 7-14. Ann Arbor, Mich.: Pierian Press, 1991.

———. *Seeking Meaning: A Process Approach to Library and Information Services.* Norwood, N.J.: Ablex, 1993.

La Guardia, Cheryl, and Christine K. Oka. *Becoming a Library Teacher.* The New Library Series, no. 3. New York: Neal-Schuman, 2000.

Laverty, Corinne. "The Cooperative Jigsaw: A New Approach to Library Learning," In *New Ways of "Learning the Library"—and Beyond: Papers and Sessions Material Presented at the Twenty-third National LOEX Library Instruction Conference Held in Denton, Texas, 5 to 6 May 1995*, edited by Linda Shirato, Elizabeth R. Bucciarelli, and Heidi Mercado, 113-23. Ann Arbor, Mich.: Pierian Press, 1996.

Lederer, Naomi. "Alert! There is a Lack of Privacy on the Web." *Academic Exchange Quarterly*, Fall 2000: 74-5.

———. "Designing Effective Research Assignments." Colorado State University Libraries. http://lib.colostate.edu/howto/instr.html

————. "How to Evaluate a Book." Colorado State University Libraries. http://lib.colostate.edu/howto/evalbk.html

————. "How to Evaluate a Web Page." Colorado State University Libraries. http://lib.colostate.edu/howto/evalweb.html

————. "How to Evaluate Journal Articles." Colorado State University Libraries. http://lib.colostate.edu/howto/evaljrl.html

————. "Library Publications Policy: Guidelines for Publications Displayed in the Arizona State University Libraries." 1992. ERIC document ED 357 757.

————. "New Form(at): Using the Web to Teach Research and Critical Thinking Skills." *Reference Services Review* 28, no. 2 (2000): 130-53.

————. "Notes to Instructors on Writing Good Research Assignments." Colorado State University Libraries. http://lib.colostate.edu/howto/instr2.html

————. "Teaching the Library and Electronic Resources on Television." In *"LOEX" of the West: Teaching and Learning in a Climate of Constant Change*, Foundations in Library and Information Science, vol. 34, edited by Thomas W. Leonhardt, 171-95. Greenwich, CT: JAI Press, 1996.

Lee, Debra S. "What Teachers Can Do to Relieve Problems Identified by International Students." In *Approaches to Teaching Non-Native English Speakers across the Curriculum*, New Directions for Teaching and Learning, no. 70, edited by David L. Sigsbee, Bruce W. Speck, and Bruce Maylath, 93-100. San Francisco: Jossey-Bass, 1997.

Loertsher, David V., and Blandch Woolls, *Information Literacy: A Review of the Literature: A Guide for Practitioners and Researcher*. 2nd ed. San Jose, Calif.: Hi Willow Research, 2002.

LOEX Clearinghouse for Library Instruction. http://www.emich.edu/public/loex/ loex.html (accessed May 18, 2004).

Loomis, Abigail, and Deborah Fink. "Meta-Learning: A Transformational Process for Learning and Teaching," In *New Ways of "Learning the Library"—and Beyond: Papers and Sessions Material Presented at the Twenty-third National LOEX Library Instruction Conference Held in Denton, Texas, 5 to 6 May 1995,* edited by Linda Shirato, Elizabeth R. Bucciarelli, and Heidi Mercado, 19-25. Ann Arbor, Mich.: Pierian Press, 1996.

Louw, Antoni A. "Break Your Barriers and Be a Better Presenter." Catherine M. Petrini, ed. "Training 101: Stage Fright." *Training & Development*, February 1992: 17, 19, 20, 22.

Marschark, Marc, Harry G. Lang, and John A. Albertini. *Educating Deaf Students: From Research to Practice.* Oxford: Oxford University Press, 2002.

McKeachie, Wilbert J. *Teaching Tips: A Guidebook for the Beginning College Teacher.* 7th ed. Lexington, Mass.: D.C. Heath, 1978.

McNulty, Tom, ed. *Accessible Libraries on Campus: A Practical Guide for the Creation of Disability-Friendly Libraries.* Chicago: American Library Association, 1999.

Meilach, Dona Z. "Overhead Transparencies Designed to Communicate." *Arts & Activities,* May 1992: 42-3, 50, 52, 56.

Mindell, Phyllis. *A Woman's Guide to the Language of Success: Communicating with Confidence and Power.* Englewood Cliffs, N.J.: Prentice Hall, 1995.

Moreton, Susie, and Fiona Salisbury. "Staying On Top of the Heap: Information Literacy and Professional Development." http://elvis.cqu.edu.au/conference/2000/papers/ moreton.htm (accessed December 24, 2003).

Myers, Isabel Briggs. Rev. by Linda K. Kirby and Katharine D. Myers. *Introduction to Type: A Guide to Understanding Your Results on the* Myers-Briggs Type Indicator®. 6th ed. Palo Alto, Calif.: Consulting Psychologists Press, 1998.

National Cancer Institute. "Research-Based Web Design & Usability Guidelines." http://www.usability.gov/guidelines/index.html (accessed January 8, 2004).

Nelson, Gayle L. "How Cultural Differences Affect Written and Oral Communication: The Case of Peer Response Groups." In *Approaches to Teaching Non-Native English Speakers across the Curriculum*, New Directions for Teaching and Learning, no. 70, edited by David L. Sigsbee, Bruce W. Speck, and Bruce Maylath, 77-84. San Francisco: Jossey-Bass, 1997.

Newstrom, John W., and Edward Scannell, *The Big Book of Presentation Games: Wake-Em-Up Tricks, Ice Breakers, & Other Fun Stuff.* New York: McGraw-Hill, 1998.

Nielsen, Jakob. "Why You Only Need to Test with 5 Users." http://www.useit.com/alertbox/20000319.htm (accessed September 20, 2003).

Niemeyer, Daniel. *Hard Facts on Smart Classroom Design: Ideas, Guidelines, and Layouts.* Lanham, Md.: Scarecrow Press, 2003.

Nilson, Linda B. *Teaching at Its Best: A Research-Based Resource for College Instruction.* Bolton, Mass.: Anker, 1998.

North, Joan DeGuire. "Put Your Money Where Your Mouth Is: A Case Study." In *The Importance of Physical Space in Creating Supportive Learning Environments*, New Directions for Teaching and Learning, no. 92, edited by Nancy Van Note Chism and Deborah J. Bickford, 73-80. San Francisco: Jossey-Bass, 2002.

Novinger, Tracy. *Intercultural Communication: A Practical Guide.* Austin: University of Texas Press, 2001.

Office of Faculty and TA Development. *Teaching in the United States: A Handbook for International Faculty and TAs 2002.* Ohio State University, 2002. Updated 26 Nov. 2001. http://ftad.osu.edu/Publications/InternationalHandbook/PDFChapterlinks.html (accessed May 16, 2004).

Osborne, Nancy Seale, and Andrea Wyman. "The Forest and the Trees: A Modest Proposal on Bibliographic Burnout." *Research Strategies* 9 (1991): 101-3.

Pack, Nancy C., and Donald D. Foos. "Library Compliance with the Americans with Disabilities Act." *RQ* 32, no. 2 (1992): 255-67.

Packard, Nick, and Phil Race, eds. *2000 Tips for Teachers.* London: Kogan Page, 2000.

Patoff, Anne M. "Redesigning the Library Web Site: Implications for Instructions." In *Library User Education in the New Millennium: Blending Tradition, Trends, and Innovation: Papers Presented at the Twenty-seventh National LOEX Library Instruction Conference Held in Houston, Texas, 11 to 13 March 1999*, edited by Julia K. Nims and Ann Andres, 115-19. Ann Arbor, Mich.: Pierian Press, 2001.

Pederson, Ann. "Teaching Over an Interactive Video Network." In *The Impact of Technology on Library Instruction: Papers and Session Materials Presented at the Twenty-first National LOEW Library Instruction Conference Held in Racine, Wisconsin, 14 to 15 May 1993*, edited by Linda Sharato, 187-91. Ann Arbor, Mich.: Pierian Press, 1995.

Perkins, David V., and Renee N. Saris. "A 'Jigsaw Classroom' Technique for Undergraduate Statistics Courses." *Teaching of Psychology*, May 2001: 111-13.

Perloff, Richard M. *The Dynamics of Persuasion: Communication and Attitudes in the 21st Century.* 2nd ed. Mahwah, N.J.: Lawrence Erlbaum, 2003.

Persons, Hal, with Lianne Mercer. *The How-to of Great Speaking: Techniques to Tame Those Butterflies.* Austin, Tex.: Black & Taylor, 1991.

Pollark, Judy P., and Paul D. Freda. "Humor, Learning, and Socialization in Middle Level Classrooms." *Clearing House,* March/April 1997: 176- [3 pages]. *Academic Search Premier,* Colorado State University Libraries. http://web8.epnet.com/ (accessed May 8, 2004).

Race, Phil. *500 Tips on Group Learning.* London: Kogan Page, 2000.

————. *The Lecturer's Toolkit: A Practical Guide to Learning, Teaching & Assessment.* 2nd ed. London: Kogan Page, 2001.

Race, Phil, and Brenda Smith. *500 Tips for Trainers.* Houston, Tex.: Gulf, 1996.

Ralph, Edwin G. *Motivating Teaching in Higher Education: A Manual for Faculty Development.* Stillwater, Okla.: New Forums Press, 1998.

Reyes, Awilda, and Naomi Lederer. "Bilingual Outreach: 'Research for Teens' on an Academic Web Site." *The Reference Librarian* 82 (2003): 141-55.

Rotondo, Jennifer, and Mike Rotondo Jr. *Presentation Skills for Managers.* New York: McGraw-Hill Briefcase Book, 2002.

Royse, David. *Teaching Tips for College and University Instructors: A Practical Guide.* Boston: Allyn and Bacon, 2001.

Ryan, Katherine E., ed. *Evaluating Teaching in Higher Education: A Vision for the Future,* New Directions for Teaching and Learning, no. 83. San Francisco: Jossey-Bass, 2000.

Sabath, Ann Marie. *International Business Etiquette: Europe: What You Need to Know to Conduct Business Abroad with Charm and Savvy.* Franklin Lakes, N.J.: Career Press,1999.

————. *International Business Etiquette: Latin America: What You Need to Know to Conduct Business Abroad with Charm and Savvy.* Franklin Lakes, N.J.: Career Press, 2000.

Sampson, Eleri. *Creative Business Presentations: Inventive Ideas for Making an Instant Impact.* London: Kogan Page, 2003.

Sarkisian, Ellen. *Teaching American Students: A Guide for International Faculty and Teaching Assistants in Colleges and Universities.* Rev. ed. Cambridge, Mass.: Derek Bok Center for Teaching and Learning, 1997.

Schoenfeld, A. Clay, and Robert Magnan. *Mentor in a Manual: Climbing the Academic Ladder to Tenure.* 2nd ed. Madison, Wis.: Atwood, 1994.

Schroeder, Charles C. "New Students—New Learning Styles." *Change* 25, no. 5 (1993): 21- . http://www.virtualschool.edu/mon/Academia/KierseyLearningStyles.html (accessed May 26, 2004).

Sheesley, Deborah F. "Burnout and the Academic Teaching Librarian: An Examination of the Problem and Suggested Solutions." *Journal of Academic Librarianship* 27, no. 6 (2001): 447-51.

Sheesley, Deborah F., moderator. "The One-Shot Multiple Section Freshman Instruction Session: Keeping the Teaching Librarian Stress-Free and Intellectually Stimulted." In *First Impressions, Lasting Impact: Introducing the First-Year Student to the Academic Library: Papers Presented at the Twenty-eighth National LOEX Library Instruction Conference held in Ypsilanti, Michigan, 19 to 20 May 2000,* edited by Julia K. Dims, 153-5. Ann Arbor, Mich.: Pierian Press, 2002.

Smith, Kitty. *Serving the Difficult Customer: A How-to-Do-It Manual for Library Staff.* How-to-Do-It Manuals for Libraries 39. New York: Neal-Schuman, 1993.

Smith, Susan Sharpless. *Web-Based Instruction: A Guide for Libraries.* Chicago: American Library Association, 2001.

Stalker, James C. "My Language, My Culture: International Variations in Standards for English." In *Approaches to Teaching Non-Native English Speakers across the Curriculum,* New Directions for Teaching and Learning, no. 70, edited by David L. Sigsbee, Bruce W. Speck, and Bruce Maylath, 7-16. San Francisco: Jossey-Bass, 1997.

Stewart-Allen, Allyson, and Lanie Denslow. *Working with Americans.* London: Pearson Education, 2002.

Strasser, Dennis. "Tips for Good Electronic Presentations," *Online,* January/February 1996: 78- [4 pages]. *Academic Search Premier,* Colorado State University Libraries. http://web8.epnet.com/ (accessed May 12, 2004).

Stronge, James H. *Qualities of Effective Teachers.* Alexandra, Va.: Association for Supervision and Curriculum Development, 2002.

Sutherland, Tracey E., and Charles C. Bonwell, eds. *Using Active Learning in College Classes: A Range of Options for Faculty,* New Directions for Teaching and Learning, no. 67. San Francisco: Jossey-Bass, 1996.

Tebbutt, David. "Presentations Made Perfect." *Director,* October 2003: 46.

Tileston, Donna Walker. *What Every Teacher Should Know about Instructional Planning.* Thousand Oaks, Calif.: Corwin Press, 2004.

———. *What Every Teacher Should Know about Learning, Memory, and the Brain.* Thousand Oaks, Calif.: Corwin Press, 2004.

Torrence, David R. "Training with Television." *Performance & Instruction* 33, no. 3 (1994): 26-9.

Tricarico, Mary Ann, Susan von Daum Tholl, and Elena O'Malley. "Interactive Online Instruction for Library Research: The Small Academic Library Experience." *Journal of Academic Librarianship* 27, no. 3 (2001): 220-3.

Tufte, Edward. *The Cognitive Style of PowerPoint.* Cheshire, Conn., 2003.

Turner, Diane, and Thelma Greco. *The Personality Compass: A New Way to Understand People.* Boston: Element, 1998.

Urech, Elizabeth. *Speaking Globally: Effective Presentations Across International and Cultural Boundaries.* Dover, N.H.: Kogan Page, 1998.

Walters, Lilly. *What to Say When . . . You're Dying on the Platform: A Complete Resource for Speakers, Trainers, and Executives.* New York: McGraw-Hill, 1995.

Weissman, Barry. "Training Low-Tech Style." *Industrial Safety & Hygiene News,* November 2002: 30-1.

Weissman, Jerry. *Presenting to Win: The Art of Telling Your Story.* Upper Saddle River, N.J.: Financial Times Prentice Hall, 2003.

White, Gayle Webb. "Teachers' Report of How They Used Humor with Students Perceived Use of Such Humor." *Education* 122, no. 2 (2001): 337-47.

Williams, Robin. *The Non-Designer's Design Book: Design and Typographic Principles for the Visual Novice.* 2nd ed. Berkeley, Calif.: Peachpit Press, 2004.

Willis, Mark R. *Dealing with Difficult People in the Library.* Chicago: American Library Association, 1999.

Woods, Peter. "Coping at School through Humor." *British Journal of Sociology of Education* 4, no. 2 (1983): 111-24.

Wriston, Henry M. *Academic Procession: Reflections of a College President.* New York: Columbia University Press, 1959.

Young, Rosemary M., and Stephena Harmony. *Working with Faculty to Design Undergraduate Information Literacy Programs: A How-to-Do-It Manual for Librarians*, How-to-Do-It Manuals for Librarians 90. New York: Neal-Schuman, 1999.

Index

About the Author

Naomi Lederer has more than seventeen years of experience teaching library instruction sessions (basic to advanced). Between 1997 and 2003 she taught an average of seventy sessions per year. She has written numerous general research strategy and how to evaluate Web pages. Individual pages on the site are linked to from over eight countries; many of the pages on the site are viewed weekly. Her subject Web pages for English, history, communication (journalism), and speech are also viewed weekly. She has taught credit library research courses in the classroom and via live cable television. By request, she has created library instruction "lectures" for distance education courses offered via WebCT (PowerPoint and audio). One of her major interests in research is the evaluation of the information once researchers find it. She has published articles (a few of them co-authored) in *Reference Services Review, The Reference Librarian, Academic Exchange Quarterly, College & Research Libraries News*, and *American Libraries*, has chapters in books, and has presented at library and education conferences in the United States, Canada, and Spain on various library topics.